BREAKTHROUGH

BREAKTHROUGH

Israel in a Changing World

Gad Yaacobi

A Herzl Press Book
•
Cornwall Books
New York • London

Cornwall Books
440 Forsgate Drive
Cranbury, NJ 08512

Cornwall Books
16 Barter Street
London WC1A 2AH, England

Cornwall Books
P.O. Box 338, Port Credit
Mississauga, Ontario
Canada L5G 4L8

Herzl Press
515 Park Avenue
New York, NY 10022

The paper used in this publication meets the requirements of the American National Standard for Permanence of Paper for Printed Library Materials Z39.48-1984.

Library of Congress Cataloging-in-Publication Data

Yaacobi, Gad, 1935–
Breakthrough : Israel in a changing world / Gad Yaacobi.
p. cm.
Includes index.
ISBN 0-8453-4858-2 (alk. paper)
1. Israel—Foreign relations. 2. Jewish-Arab relations—1973–
I. Title.
DS119.6.Y324 1996
327.5694—dc20
95-51994
CIP

PRINTED IN THE UNITED STATES OF AMERICA

Dedicated to the memory of the late Prime Minister of Israel, Mr. Yitzhak Rabin. A courageous soldier. A victorious commander. A historic statesman. A friend. A warrior who fell in the battle for peace.

To Nella, my partner in the breakthrough, who has stood by me with charm and devotion.

Contents

Introduction

THIS book is a compilation of speeches, articles, and essays exploring aspects of Israel-UN relations, Israel-Diaspora relations, progress toward peace, and the enormous potential for change in the Middle East.

The period covered was one of revolutionary change. The speed and scope of developments took many by surprise, but so quickly became a part of the new reality that the word *change* itself became, in a sense, banal.

Of course, the upheavals in the international arena were not limited to the Middle East. The United Nations, in this period, began a substantial review of its outlook and role for the post-cold war era. As a result, it has increased its involvement in global affairs—politically, economically, socially, culturally, and environmentally. But heightened expectations also generated deep disappointments with the organization's shortcomings and failures. The UN system and its member states continue to try to apply the lessons learned, and to redefine the role and priorities of the United Nations for the coming decades.

In the period that I have been serving as Israeli Ambassador to the UN, we have crossed a watershed in the Middle East and in Israel's international standing.

The manifestations of this watershed are diverse. Among them, broadening cooperation with the member states and Secretariat of the United Nations, with its agencies and peacekeeping forces. Likewise, far-reaching, positive changes have been made in General Assembly resolutions relating to the Middle East and Israel. Israeli candidates have been elected to various posts in the UN system, and other Israelis have been integrated into the UN's agencies, bodies and peacekeeping activities.

These are some of the first fruits of the end of Cold War, the beginning of the Middle East peace process, and the emergence of new geopolitical structures. They also stem from the new directions in Israeli foreign policy and domestic priorities.

Immediately upon assuming my post as ambassador in September 1992, I made clear that our goal was nothing less than the normalization of Israel's relationship with the United Nations, its bodies, and agencies, through cooperation with every willing member state and participation in every facet of UN activities. Over the past two and a half years, we have made substantial progress toward meeting this goal. Considering the situation in the past, a significant, dramatic change. I firmly believe that this change will continue.

Since signing the Declaration of Principles with the Palestinians, we have established diplomatic relations with twenty-seven countries, in addition to forging formal ties with Morocco and Tunisia and cooperative relationships with other countries. Israel now has formal relations with 155 countries out of the 185 UN member states.

We have increased our involvement in the deliberations of the General Assembly and other UN organs. We also maintain good working relationships with representatives of almost all countries in the UN, including those with which we do not have formal diplomatic relations.

The experience of maintaining a continued dialogue with ambassadors from cultures so different from our own, each representing his or her own country's unique perspective and particular interests, is fascinating. There is no doubt that the personal contact carries a not insignificant weight in the ability of nations to promote their separate and shared interests. The system of frequent formal and informal dialogue that characterizes life at the United Nations produces changes in countries' positions as well as continued practical relations between states.

From the outset, I have viewed myself as have most of my predecessors, Abba Eban, Yosef Tekoa, Chaim Herzog, Yehuda Blum, and Binyamin Netanyahu, as one whose mission it is also to maintain a dialogue with the Jewish communities of the Western Hemisphere. I have met Jewish groups throughout the United States, Canada, and South America. The partnership between the Jews in Diaspora and Israel is, in my opinion, the backbone both of Israel's future and of the continued Jewish identification of Diaspora Jews. Developments in both communities and in the world at large have shaken up the old frameworks of Israel-Diaspora relations, and both sides are now searching for a redefinition.

To represent Israel before the international community at this time of replacing old, broken models with new—but untested—ones and to be a partner in the great breakthrough in our international and regional standing are great undertakings and responsibilities for me. I also view it as an additional stage in my lifelong career serving the national and public welfare. I was born in Eretz Yisrael, to Jewish parents who immigrated for ideological reasons from Byelorussia and Ukraine in 1923, during the Third Aliyah. They founded a *moshav,* a cooperative village, where I was born and where I spent my childhood. Upon my release from the army and the completion of my studies in university, I naturally entered national and public service, first in the Ministry of Agriculture and later as a member of Knesset, the Israeli Parliament, and a minister in Israeli governments, where I participated in making decisions affecting the very future of Israel, in the security, foreign affairs, economic, and social realms.

I see my current position as the logical extension of my prior work. My experience helps me to understand the considerations that drive Israeli policy. Throughout my work in the multilateral institution known as the UN, I have relied upon my Knesset and ministerial experience. It has been of great benefit to me here as well as to my ability to maintain a constructive dialogue with the Jewish communities of North and South America.

I hope that this book will contribute to a better understanding of the subjects addressed, and I hope it will provoke thought and discussion.

I wish to thank Avner Tavori, Shaul Kelner, Michael Freund, and Brad Rothschild for their help in preparing this book. I would also like to express my appreciation to Sam Bloch, the head of Herzl Press, for his assistance in publishing the collection in such a fine arrangement and to Arie Hecht for the excellent jacket.

GAD YAACOBI
Israeli Ambassador to the United Nations

New York
November 1995, Kislev 5756

* * * * * * * * *

After this book was completed, the State of Israel experienced a tragic and traumatic event, the assassination of Prime Minister Yitzhak Rabin. Rabin, together with Shimon Peres, initiated the breakthrough in the Middle East. As a result of their vision, Israel has benefited from far-reaching changes in its relationship with the international community.

Only a week before his death, the Prime Minister was in New York to participate in the Special Session of the General Assembly

Commemorating the Fiftieth Anniversary of the United Nations. During his five-day visit, Rabin met with leaders from thirty-five nations; had there been more time, he surely would have met with many others. The reception that was extended to Yitzhak Rabin by the leaders of the global community is an indication of the monumental changes in Israel's international standing that Rabin's policies helped bring about.

Yitzhak Rabin always referred to himself as "a simple soldier." Yet, he was a soldier in service of the Jewish nation and the State of Israel; most of all, he was a soldier for peace and security.

I believe that Yitzhak Rabin's legacy, along with the commitment and rich experience of Shimon Peres, will enable Israel to the enhance the peace process and fulfill his vision.

BREAKTHROUGH

Part One
Israel among the Nations

1

New World Disorder

An Agenda for Peace

As this is my first address in the General Assembly of the United Nations, I would like to greet all of you, the President, the Secretary-General, and the representatives and delegates of all Member States, with the traditional Israeli greeting of shalom, which means "peace."

The principles enshrined in the Charter of the United Nations speak eloquently of the determination, and I quote: "to save succeeding generations from the scourge of war . . . to reaffirm faith in fundamental human rights, in the dignity and worth of the human person, in the equal rights of men and women and of nations . . . to practice tolerance and live together in peace with one another as good neighbors, and to unite our strength to maintain international peace and security . . . and to employ international machinery for the promotion of the economic and social advancement of all peoples. . . ."

Events in the world today present us with many challenges, and we must address the following questions courageously:

> "Are the words of the Charter merely words, words, words?
>
> What is our duty to stop the killing in Bosnia? to halt terrorism? to enhance democracies rather than totalitarian regimes? to free the world from hunger?
>
> To put it simply: Are we truly committed to carrying out the Charter of the United Nations?

If the answer is no, then we must confront the Greek orator Demosthenes' question: "What greater crime can an orator be charged with, than that his opinions and his language are not the same?"

The Secretary-General's report "An Agenda for Peace" is a courageous proposal to truly grapple with our commitment to peace and freedom, as it was inscribed in the charter.

We in Israel are ready and willing to take an active part in creating a new political environment. As Foreign Minister Shimon Peres stated before this Assembly on 1 October 1992: "The United Nations was established in an era that no longer exists. Yet its ideals and structures can meet the challenges and dangers of this new age. We support the agenda for peace offered by the Secretary-General."

A new reality has emerged in the global arena, and we must address it. No longer is this organization shackled by the chains of superpower rivalry. With the end of the Cold War, a new kind of United Nations is being formed and molded. The United Nations must now be a leading force, based on agreement among member states that the only escape from hunger, from misery and from bloodshed is peaceful, cultured relations among peoples and nations. That was the vision of the biblical prophets, and that is what is needed for the next millennium, which is at our doorstep.

As we seek to construct a brighter future, it is imperative that we be guided by the light of peace and democracy. Many states are putting their resources, their human energies, and their creativity to waste by continuing to pursue military and other types of conflict. If all those resources would instead be devoted to investment in human capital and economic development, we could be improving lives rather than ending them. If we invest in health, education, and science instead of military hardware, then within one generation mankind could be free from hunger and illiteracy. The choice before us is between a barren future and a better future.

The other key to mankind's progress is democracy, namely, the participation of people in defining their own lives and their own future. Without democracy there cannot be an environment of human rights. It is a fallacy to think that human rights can be safeguarded by totalitarian regimes and military dictatorships.

Democracy is an essential component of maintaining peaceful relations among states. The existence of a democratic government is the central guarantee for preventing a policy of violence and aggression. Never has one democracy declared war upon another democracy. This is not a result of chance; rather, it is a result of the nature of democracies. Therefore, democratization is not just a political and moral issue, but rather is directly tied to the existence of peace and stability.

Peace and democracy are the keys to a better world. This must be stated firmly and clearly. It is the basic and solid truth, and all of us must acknowledge it.

The Middle East might be called "the land of lost opportunities." Lost opportunities have carried a very heavy and painful price for the peoples of the Middle East. Now we have a historic opportunity to change the situation; to create a new and better future for all of us; to replace tension with economic development, war with peace, and rearmament with investment in human resources.

Egypt and Israel have so far been the only countries in the Middle East who have courageously not missed the opportunity for peace. Now, a new window of opportunity has been opened. Bilateral negotiations are currently being held between Israel and the neighboring Arab states, and the Palestinians. We hope that these negotiations will lead to peace treaties, and we hope that Syria, Jordan, Lebanon, the Palestinians, and Israel will not miss this historic moment.

In light of recent events, I call for an end to provocative acts of violence by extremists. We can not afford to allow them to murder the prospects for peace.

No provocation will divert Israel from the peace track. But Israel stands by its right to defend its citizens with its full force and authority.

The bilateral talks as well as the multilateral negotiations have created a new dynamic with good prospects. If there is a breakthrough towards a peace treaty between Israel and Syria, this will be the engine that will lead to a change in the face of the entire Middle East. Even if this does not occur, the train will have to go on. We shall not allow the steam to go with the wind.

An important and encouraging development, even revolutionary in the history of nations in the Middle East, is the growing awareness of the interdependence among peace, economic development, and the general well-being of people in the region.

Peace is therefore likely to be a great lever to regional economic development. The United Nations, the United States, Russia, the Europeans, Canada, Japan, and others can mobilize their expertise and resources in numerous fields, including the establishment of a Middle East Development Bank. A peaceful environment could free $30 billion annually from the cost of defense for progress and development. Moreover, it will also gradually allow six major new directions:

- the establishment of a Middle Eastern Common Market;
- the creation of joint ventures, based upon integrated knowl-

edge, capital, and mineral resources from both inside and outside the region;

- the establishment of an integrated network of infrastructure for ports, airports, railways, and energy plants;
- the opening of borders for tourism;
- the promotion of cooperation in the fields of health, professional training, knowledge, technology, and agriculture;
- the removal of all sorts of boycotts.

Peace and democracy are the key elements to mankind's progress. As such, I would like to raise the idea of initiating two task forces under the authority of the Secretary-General. One task force would be devoted to encouraging democratization through education about democracy and free elections. The goal of the United Nations Task Force on Democracy would be to create a new state of mind regarding the importance of democracy for ensuring human rights and for improving the quality of life of people.

A second proposed task force would seek to initiate regional cooperation in different parts of the world. It might be based upon the experience of the European Community and other regional frameworks for cooperation. Regional cooperation is necessary to enhance the ability of developing countries to cope with the more developed and wealthier countries of the world.

All great achievements in human history were dreams before they became realities. Our task as statesmen is to translate the dreams into reality. David Ben-Gurion, the founder and first leader of my country, said, "Israel's future will be determined by its righteousness and strength." With regard to this Assembly, I would like to state that: our ability to fulfill our duty will be determined by our righteousness, strength, and dedication to the vision and cause of peace.

Excerpted from speech delivered in the United Nations General Assembly, 27 October 1992.

Human Rights and Wrongs

Today in Vienna, for the first time in twenty-five years, a World Conference on Human Rights will be convened. This is an international event of great significance, and it could very well serve to fundamentally strengthen the protection and preservation of human rights around the world. With the spread of ethnic, religious, and national conflicts, the idea of having such a conference is a welcome one. But it also has the potential of turning into a theater of the absurd, marked by surrealistic scenes of hypocrisy and double standards.

Among the participants at the conference will be representatives from various totalitarian, non-democratic, cruel and inhumane regimes. They view the conference not so much as a forum for discussing human rights, but as a means of covering up their own abuses of those very same rights. Such countries will no doubt seize upon the massive media presence to preach to others about the need to respect human rights, even as they trample upon them back home.

Sadly, it would not be the first time that such absurd ironies have occurred. It is a fact of life at the United Nations that representatives of countries such as Iraq or the Sudan, who are among the worst abusers of human rights, will ascend the podium, muster up a pretense of righteous indignation, and proceed to discourse about the failings of the West and various other democratic countries. That their own regimes rule thanks to bullets rather than ballots does not in any way inhibit them from preaching what they fail to practice.

Such countries will try to throw up a smokescreen around their own abuses. Should they succeed in doing so, it will serve only to undermine the effectiveness of the conference. Despots should not be allowed to steal the show. Their double standards should be exposed for what they are: cynical manipulations of the issue of human rights.

Very few, however, are ready to face the reality of the global human rights situation with honesty and courage. Too many are ready to just pay lip service to it instead of addressing the substance of the matter. The substance is not the symptoms of the disease, but rather the disease itself: a lack of democracy in about 135 of the 183 member states of the United Nations.

In recent years, there have been unprecedented changes as the Soviet Union collapsed, totalitarianism in Eastern Europe was swept away, and the authoritarian regimes in Latin America fell. In their place, democracy took root. But the fact remains that only a minority of countries around the world currently enjoy truly democratic systems. Most remain under the grip of feudal, repressive, or nondemocratic leaders. With the spread of extreme nationalism and xenophobia, and the consequent violations of human rights that accompany them, it is all the more crucial that steps be taken now to foster a world-wide process of democratization. The democratic countries must offer their advice, support and assistance to the emerging democracies.

The gassing of the Kurds in northern Iraq, the genocide perpetrated against Cambodians in the 1970s, and the labor camps of the Soviet gulag all resulted in part from the absence of democracy in those countries. To prevent such persecution from recurring in the future against other vulnerable minorities, it is imperative that democracy be enshrined as the governing ideology in nations across the globe. That is the message that must emerge, clearly and firmly, from the World Conference on Human Rights in Vienna. The Conference should serve as a framework for replacing lip service with truth, and slogans with substance. It is the task of the democratic countries, with the leadership of the United States, to ensure that it does.

Article originally published in *The Los Angeles Times,* 14 June 1993.

Television Shouldn't Decide Where the UN Sends Forces

More than five hundred thousand people died in 1993 as a result of the civil war in Angola. Approximately forty percent of the dead were children under the age of ten. The civil war has also orphaned four hundred thousand children and displaced three million people.

But in the United Nations, more pressing issues pushed discussions on Angola to the sidelines. UN action has been slow in coming, despite the revolutionary changes in policy that have increased UN peace-keeping forces worldwide from ten thousand soldiers in 1990 to an eighty-five thousand troop, four-billion-dollar operation today.

CNN did not go to Angola. No television network brought the pictures of this war into living rooms in America, Europe, or anywhere else. The result: the Angolan civil war never became a topic for an international drama, and the international community never made this war a priority on their agenda.

Bosnia would not have united the NATO, the United States, and Russia in action were it not for the graphic images of the slaughter in the Sarajevo marketplace. The Israeli-Palestinian conflict would not have focused world attention so much were it not for the pictures of stone throwers during the intifada. Boris Yeltsin would not have become the hero of the Western world were it not for the CNN cameras that captured him standing on a tank in front of the

Russian White House. Troops providing humanitarian aid would not have been deployed in Somalia, were it not for the haunting pictures of starving children.

The Cold War has been replaced by many hot wars raging in different focal points all over the globe. Approximately one-third of the countries in the world are embroiled in internal or regional conflicts. The UN, through its peacekeeping forces, is now involved directly in twenty-three of them.

The UN, of course, cannot and should not intervene in every national, ethnic, or religious conflict in the world. Yet when deciding which conflicts warrant international intervention, media coverage should not be our criterion for determining priorities, nor should it affect the decisions on the nature of UN involvement. In the case of Somalia, the UN and the United States were obligated to extend humanitarian aid. But under pressure created by the media, this mission was extended to transforming a tribal society into a modern democracy. Sending 25,000 soldiers on Operation Restore Hope to provide humanitarian aid was justified, but leaving them there for the purposes of "nation building" was a naive mistake.

The UN, United States, and especially the Europeans, waited too long before any action was taken to stop, or at least limit, the war in Bosnia and the murder of the Moslems there. The media generated pressure on the leaders of the world to send in troops, or at least start air strikes, and so to intervene in the civil war. (I was once told by another ambassador that CNN is like the sixteenth member of the fifteen-member Security Council.) However, based on the lessons learned in Somalia, the UN and NATO did not yield to the popular demand to become active participants in the fighting. Rather, they issued an ultimatum from the outside to remove the heavy weapons. In this way, the UN and NATO succeeded in removing the artillery surrounding Sarajevo without direct intervention in the civil war.

The United Nations and the international community have been successful when they have offered peacekeeping forces that contribute to security and help supervise agreements. Two good examples are United Nations Disengagement Observer Force, which monitors the Israeli-Syrian agreement on disengagement of forces, and the Multinational Force in Sinai, whose role is to ensure that no armies move into the demilitarized zone created by the Camp David Accords.

The UN has also been successful when their mission was limited to humanitarian aid. It is because of this that when Israel was examining avenues of participation in peacekeeping operations, it decided to become involved only in humanitarian and civilian areas. We are considering operating a field hospital in one of the African countries that hosts or will host UN peacekeepers. We are also willing to assist in civilian training in other locations.

The decision to participate in peacekeeping operations was taken as a demonstration of our new relationship with the international community and of the changes and developments that have occurred in UN-Israel relations: substantial changes in General Assembly resolutions, a positive stance toward the peace process, cooperation with UN bodies and agencies, and diplomatic relations with 140 out of 184 UN member states. Beyond this, our decision is based upon a strategic conception of the role of peacekeeping forces in the world today.

In the new world disorder, the international community has to reexamine the guidelines for UN peacekeeping and redefine its priorities in this regard. We cannot tolerate a situation in which television coverage is the leading factor, sometimes the only factor, in deciding which conflicts deserve resources, attention, and peacekeepers. This has been the case in many instances until now, and the time has come for a change.

Article originally published in *The Philadelphia Inquirer*, 25 March 1994.

Still No Peace On Earth

The sense that the world is turning towards the path of peace is felt most dramatically when we consider the historic changes in South Africa, the thaw in our relations with Middle Eastern countries such as Morocco, Jordan, and some of the Gulf states, and the advancing peace process with the Palestinians, Syrians, and others.

Larger processes of economic and political integration in various parts of the world reinforce that sense. For example, the European Parliament's decision to extend membership to Austria, Sweden, Finland, and Norway, creates a European Union comprising sixteen member states with a combined population of 370 million (compared with six members when the Common Market was established in 1957). The NAFTA agreement creates an economic union between the United States, Canada, and Mexico, and other regions are undergoing similar developments as well.

Yet in spite of this, peace on earth is a dream that is sadly retreating farther and farther away. True, the end of the Cold War has lessened the danger of nuclear confrontation between the superpowers; however, the world now finds itself in yet another period of bloodshed and war.

Approximately fifty violent conflicts, regional and internal, are raging in the world today. Since the beginning of 1993, they have claimed the lives of over two million people: in Angola, almost a half million; in Rwanda during the last few months alone, almost two hundred thousand; in Yemen and in the former Yugoslavia, tens of thousands. And recently, the war over Kashmir between India and Pakistan flared up again. The list goes on.

Most of these conflicts are ethnic or religious. Some are long-standing, as in the Balkans, Northern Ireland, Pakistan, India, China, and Peru. Some are newer, stemming from the end of Soviet domination in parts of Europe and Asia—as in Azerbaijan and Afghanistan. Some ride the crest of a rising tide of Islamic fundamentalism—as in Algeria, Egypt, and Sudan. Some are the product of ethnic minorities' demands for self-determination—as in Kurdistan.

In the past two years, millions of people have been forcibly displaced or exiled from their homes. There are those who attribute the wars, the killing and the refugees to the end of the bipolar Cold War world, divided between the United States and the Soviet Union. They also result from the demands of ethnic and religious minorities for self-determination.

In most instances, these conflicts are occurring in and among non-democratic countries. They lack mechanisms built-in to the democratic system that diffuse tensions and produce amicable solutions to problems. Still, we have to remember that the large majority of member states of the United Nations are not democratic countries.

United Nations involvement in world conflicts via peacekeeping forces and attempts at mediation have greatly expanded in recent years. In the UN's first forty-three years from 1945 to 1988, it intervened in only thirteen conflicts (including in Lebanon, the Golan Heights and the West Bank and Gaza). In the last six years, the UN intervened in twenty-four conflicts. Now, the Security Council has decided to send forces to Rwanda and is considering sending forces to Angola as well.

****

As this occurs, we are witnessing a fundamental change in the balance of forces. A multipolar world is rising to replace the bipolar world of the Cold War. In this structure, the United States remains the dominant power. However, alongside it other powers are gaining influence, including China, Germany (the most powerful member of the European Union), and Japan. In the future, these nations will most likely be joined by Russia, Brazil, and India.

Such changes are already affecting international developments and are limiting the influence of the United States.

The world faces two great threats for the future. The first is the proliferation of weapons of mass destruction—atomic, biological, and chemical. Warring sides in certain regional conflicts, in the absence of the "balance of terror," are liable to resort to such weapons. The second is the spread of Islamic fundamentalism and other extremist religious movements that feed off a mixture of hunger and fanaticism.

In the nondemocratic world, flooded with advanced technologies of mass destruction and steeped in religious fanaticism and ethnic and tribal rivalries, peace is still a distant dream.

This is the New World Disorder, and it is the basis for the United States' post-Cold War foreign policy. The pivotal point at which the world will choose its direction—toward integration and harmony or toward disintegration and conflict—will not come quickly. This is a historical process, slow and painful.

We, therefore, have to make this process of change work for us, to bring peace between ourselves and the Palestinians and neighboring countries. In so doing, we should spare no effort, not because this is a historical imperative, but because it is an historic opportunity that might never appear again. We should seize the opportunity, not for the world's sake, and not even for our neighbors' sakes, but for our own.

Article originally published in *The Washington Jewish Week*, 30 June 1994.

A New Age of Uncertainty

An emerging black market in the smuggling and sale of plutonium from the former Soviet Union, human tragedy in Rwanda, a threatened invasion of Haiti, international terrorism and disintegrating regimes in Africa—all have captured the world's attention via global media and international conferences. Yet the common denominator unifying these developments seems unclear.

Contrary to most assumptions and expectations, the world finds itself in an age of growing uncertainty. Who predicted the collapse of the Soviet Union? The Gulf War? By now, it is clear that we should expect the unexpected. At the same time that economic unions are expanding and centralized regimes are opening up, new and unidentified dangers are looming on the horizon. Many of them may prove difficult to stop.

Despite this, the international community and even the United States have yet to define a strategy for meeting the challenges of the post-Cold War world. Lacking clear policy objectives, the floundering attempts to respond to dynamic situations have often seemed futile.

Progress toward peace has occurred in only two regions—the Middle East and South Africa. There, conditions were made ripe for accommodation only following the hardship of the parties to the conflict and their own decision that the time had come to create a new reality. No externally imposed solutions produced the agreement between Israel and the PLO, or Israel and Jordan. The same is true of South Africa. In every conflict where the international community or the United States has tried to impose a solution on unwilling parties, failure has been inevitable. So it was in Somalia. So it is in Rwanda and Bosnia.

The United Nations Security Council has given a green light to the American initiative regarding Haiti. But the prospects of an invasion to impose democracy seem more and more doubtful. To many, such an invasion would seem to ignore the lessons taught by recent interventions.

Five principal threats endanger the world today. Confronting them will require broader strategies than previously conceived. None can be solved by merely sending in the calvary.

- Islamic fundamentalism—A driving force behind much of the international terrorism in the world today. Islamic fundamentalism is spreading throughout Arab and African countries and will continue to pose a threat to their stability and to Western security until the social misery and economic stagnation it thrives on are eliminated.
- Ethnic, religious, national, and tribal conflicts—There are approximately fifty such conflicts raging throughout the world today—the greatest number since the end of World War II. In

the past year and a half alone, they have claimed the lives of more than three million people.

- Nuclear proliferation—The spread of nuclear weapons is made even more difficult to prevent due to the open market for nuclear experts and know-how, the sale of plutonium to the highest bidder, and the subsequent creation of nuclear programs, in some cases by countries whose responsibility and restraint are in serious doubt.
- Exploding populations. Population growth is skyrocketing in Africa, South America, and parts of Asia. With it come poverty, starvation, epidemics, and massive waves of refugees. All this generates enormous human suffering and dangerous political instability.
- Nondemocratic regimes—The minority of countries in the world are run by democratic governments. Of the 184 states in the United Nations, only about fifty can be defined as democracies. The combination of nuclear proliferation, fundamentalist terrorism, and a nondemocratic majority in the world holds the potential for an exceedingly dangerous future for us all.

The international community, led by the United States, must develop a strategy for meeting the challenges of the coming decades. To be effective, such a strategy will have to address the root causes of the major new threats to world stability. Yet it is hard to discern even the beginnings of an attempt to shape a comprehensive policy for this new age of uncertainty.

Based on the Hebrew article originally published in *Ha'aretz,* 30 August 1994.

Agenda for Development

The United Nations Agenda for Development will likely determine the fate of the world: Will we descend deeper into the spiral of world disorder, wars, genocide, and human suffering, or will we shape a better future for all people?

Many factors will contribute: religious and tribal fanaticism, national psyches scarred by past traumas, totalitarian regimes, selfish interests, and more. All these might play a negative part in determining the future of human society in the next century. But a decisive positive role can be played by economic, social, scientific, and technological progress.

Current trends give cause for concern.

- World population is expanding at a dramatic pace, especially in developing areas. Demographers expect that world population, currently 5.7 billion people, will soar to between 7.6 billion and 9.4 billion by 2025. Almost 95 percent of this growth will take place in developing countries. In these countries, it is already difficult to meet the needs of the existing population with the limited resources at hand.
- Disparities between different parts of the world continue to grow: between North and South, between democratic countries and nondemocratic countries, between more educated societies and less educated ones.
- Hunger, shortages, and economic depression are causing enormous human suffering. They are starving people of hope, while feeding conflicts and radicalism—religious, national, tribal, and military.

The price is paid first and foremost by the people in the afflicted countries. But it also takes a toll on the entire international community.

The roots of the problem are already clear.

- Low levels of education prevent too many societies from realizing their full potential.
- Billions of dollars that could be spent on development are wasted on armies and weapons. The excessiveness of these expenditures is made even more clear when we consider *per capita* spending. The historian Paul Kennedy described the probable outcome in his book, *The Rise and Fall of the Great Powers*. History has shown that countries that labored under burdensome defense budgets and continued military involvement became second-rate societies, economically and socially stagnant.
- Most states still do not enjoy democratic systems and the benefits they bring. The standard of living in democratic societies is the highest in the world, because they produce pluralistic, open, and enterprising economies. In recent years, some progress has been made toward greater democratization throughout the world but most countries and peoples still do not enjoy democracy.

- Corruption and abuse of excessive power by the few prevents an improvement in the human condition of the many.
- Throughout much of the world, infrastructure remains underdeveloped. This includes communications, transportation, energy, electricity, and water.
- Finally, too many countries suffer from a lack of integration into the regional and global economies.

The roots of the problem point clearly to the necessary solutions.

- Raise the level of education and professional training.
- Reduce military expenditures by working to achieve peace and understanding.
- Encourage democratization.
- Open up economies to all forms of entrepreneurship.
- Work for regional and international cooperation, for integration in the global economy, and for the elimination of all forms of boycotts.

Leadership is crucial to achieving these goals. The principal responsibility will fall to individual states, rulers, and public opinion leaders.

This has been proven in the Middle East. The peace treaty between Egypt and Israel, the agreements between Israel and the PLO, the peace treaty with Jordan, the establishment of formal relations with Morocco and Tunisia, and the establishment of a framework for multilateral cooperation—all these were brought about by the courage and wisdom of leaders.

Although we still face hardships and obstacles, the direction is clear: peace, regional cooperation, economic and commercial development, integrated infrastructures, and exchange of knowledge and information. In this way, the societies of the Middle East will stop wasting resources on conflicts, and instead invest them in people. The energies will be directed toward the creation of a better, more secure, and prosperous future.

The main responsibility lies with the parties involved. But the international community also has an important role in assisting to achieve these goals. So it is in the Middle East, and so it is in other regions of the world.

International financial institutions have a responsibility to assist in creating a more advanced human and physical infrastructure.

The international economic and trade system has a responsibility to assist in developing trade and economic ties.

The United Nations and its agencies—in humanitarian, social, and educational assistance.

The democratic countries—in encouraging a gradual transition to participatory societies. This should be done without coercion, through the influence of mass media, intellectuals, and business leaders.

The world is undergoing painful changes. Some of these are producing deep concerns. But these should not be a cause for despair. There is a chance for advancement. There are countries and regions that prove that positive change is possible; that the future can hold more promise instead of less. The key is held by the people and their leaders, by the international community, by all of us.

Excerpted from a speech delivered in the United Nations General Assembly, 21 November 1994.

Peace and Non-Proliferation: Which Comes First?

How can countries that failed to keep the nuclear genie in the bottle at least keep it close to the bottle? This question will be the subject of an international conference that meets this month to decide the fate of the Treaty on Nonproliferation of Nuclear Weapons (NPT), first ratified in 1968.

If the Cold War threatened a global nuclear confrontation between the superpowers, at least it kept the weapons of mass destruction in the hands of a relatively few. The post-Cold War disorder presents a different type of threat. As nervous gazes shift to North Korea, Iraq, and Iran, the possibilities of regional devastation and nuclear terrorism seem more immediate than once they did, especially when we are speaking of nondemocratic regimes.

Clearly, the nonconventional threat varies with the political landscape. Nonproliferation arrangements have to account for this.

The Middle East presents a unique case. Host to more rogue states than any other region; birthplace and hotbed of Islamic fundamentalism; home to Hamas, Hizballah, Islamic Jihad, and numerous other terrorist organizations.

In this region where dictatorship, fundamentalism, and terrorism hold sway, some countries have proven demonstrably lax in fulfilling their commitments under the NPT.

Case 1. Iraq: Signature notwithstanding, Iraq embarked on a nuclear weapons development program that was interrupted only by Israeli action in 1981, the Gulf War ten years later, and the UNSCOM regime established in the wake of the war.

Case 2. Iran: Not satisfied with spreading Islamic revolution through conventional terrorism alone, Iran's program to develop a nuclear arsenal is well under way. This, despite its signature on the NPT. US and Israeli intelligence project that even without outside help, Iran will hold a nuclear bomb in its grip within five to ten years.

Attempts to force Israel to join the NPT regime seem incongruous in this light. Moreover, considering Israel's unqualified support for the principle of nonproliferation of weapons of mass destruction, support for the indefinite and unconditional extension of the NPT, and consistent advocacy of the establishment in due course of a mutually verifiable nuclear-weapon-free zone (NWFZ), freely and directly negotiated, encompassing all states of the region.

Israel has to honestly assess its own security situation. We cannot ignore the fact that some states in the region (among them, Iran, Iraq, and Libya) consider themselves in a state of war with us and still openly advocate our destruction.

The demand that Israel sign the NPT without taking this reality into account goes against all notions of common sense. Nuclear arms control cannot be addressed in a vacuum. Fundamental questions of war, peace, and security must first be addressed, and the solutions will have to rest primarily on political accommodation.

Nuclear nonproliferation is best addressed in the full context of the peace process, following a logical, step-by-step approach. First, build the confidence that undergirds peace. Then establish peace agreements that prove their durability over time. Follow this with complementary conventional and nonconventional arms control arrangements. Finally, as the crowning achievement, negotiate a credible, mutually verifiable nuclear-weapon-free zone that encompasses all states of the region.

Arms control is supposed to enhance security, not encroach on it. We have formulated our nonproliferation policy with this in mind, always conscious of the neighborhood we live in.

Peace is the truest security. There is no substitute. A nuclear-weapon-free zone in a peaceful Middle East is our best hope to ensure that our children do not grow up with a nuclear sword of Damocles hanging over their heads.

Published in the *Jerusalem Post,* 17 April 1995.

2

Israel and the UN

A Role to Play at the UN

Economic blocs have begun crystallizing around the world, marking the beginnings of unprecedented economic integration among states.

At the same time, sources of tension and ethnic and religious conflict seem to be proliferating, from Angola to Yugoslavia to Tajikistan, and sentiment is growing in support of international intervention in many of these conflicts.

Such intervention can take different forms, from direct military intervention (the Gulf War) to "humanitarian intervention," (Somalia) or mediation (Bosnia-Herzegovina).

But whatever the form, many have begun to look to the UN to fill the need. While this might lead to frustration as a result of unrealistically high expectations, there is no better alternative.

UN Secretary-General Dr. Boutros Boutros-Ghali recently issued an ambitious and wide-ranging report entitled "An Agenda for Peace," which clearly demonstrates the expanding role of the UN. The report expressed the intentions of the UN's founding fathers, together with the current desire for increased UN involvement in conflict resolution.

There are now forty-eight conflicts raging in various part of the globe. In a number of them the UN has intensified its involvement through the use of peacekeeping forces. About ninety thousand soldiers are serving in UN peacekeeping operations, including UNIFIL and UNDOF troops on Israel's norther border.

There is no reason why Israel should confine itself at the UN solely to affairs directly relating to the Middle East. Like any other country, it should participate fully in UN debates, general activities, and projects. While our main efforts and energy must focus on achieving peace with our neighbors, increased participation in the UN can contribute to this goal.

In the General Assembly debate over the Secretary-General's report, Israel argued that the challenges facing the world today can be met only if peace and democracy are strengthened.

In these two areas, peacekeeping and democracy, Israel has a great deal to offer the international community. The growing importance of the UN and its increasingly visible role necessitates a strengthening of Israel's relationship with the organization and its member states.

Israel's position at the UN has improved markedly since the end of the Cold War, the changes in the Middle East, the beginning of direct peace negotiations, and the change in government policy as a result of the Israeli elections.

The structure of the UN does not facilitate such progress within the UN; about 110 member states are within the nonaligned movement; 37 of those are Moslem and Arab states. However, Israel now has relations with 120 of the 180 member states of the UN.

Israel is working diligently to normalize its relationship with the UN and its various agencies and to expand its cooperation with UN programs in areas such as culture (UNESCO), child welfare (UNICEF), health (WHO), and agriculture (FAO).

Israel should not view the UN as a necessarily hostile entity, but as a framework in which it can play an active role.

At a recent session of the General Assembly, a number of changes were evident. Assembly resolutions on the Middle East, the Palestinian question, Israeli nuclear armament, and the Golan Heights all showed significant and welcome changes in tone and substance.

Article originally published in *The Jerusalem Post International Edition,* 13 March 1993.

The Challenges Ahead

The role of the United Nations has changed in the last three or four years following the changes on the world scene: the end of the Cold War leaving the United States as the only remaining superpower; and the various ethnic and religious conflicts now raging in some fifty-five locations around the world. The United Nations had very little credibility in a paralyzed Cold War era. Now I think the United Nations is suffering from too great expectations in its desire to solve all the problems of the world.

The notion that internal and regional conflicts can be solved through external intervention is a very dangerous one. We saw it before in Cyprus, Lebanon, and Vietnam. A heavy price was paid for trying to solve those problems through external intervention. Such is the case in the former republics of Yugoslavia. The United Nations is involved today in many conflicts involving complicated social, political, and psychological variables, which cannot be solved through intervention by peacekeeping troops. Those countries have to pass through a long-term process of healing and negotiation until some solutions will be reached.

****

Last week in Vienna, the United Nations held a World Conference on Human Rights. One has to remember that out of 183 member states in the United Nations, 145 are nondemocratic. It is, therefore, ridiculous and surreal that an organization with an overwhelming majority of nondemocratic members who in their countries do not practice human rights at all—because human rights can only exist in democratic regimes—would address issues regarding global human rights. Perhaps this is the reason why the conference adopted a ridiculous decision guaranteeing the freedom and protection of the press, "Within the framework of national law" in each country. So Iraq within its national law and Syria, Pakistan, Libya, and Sudan within their "national law[s]" can do whatever they so choose. This is merely lip service to human rights and nothing more.

The conference was a big tourist attraction in Austria, at least this is one good thing I can say about it. Another good thing is that it also stayed away from adopting anti-Israeli resolutions. But as far as the human rights issues, it did nothing but preserve the status quo, which means doing almost nothing.

****

Israel's relations with the United Nations have changed over time. The UN accepted Israel into its fold in 1949. It also adopted the resolution of partition of Palestine that enabled the formation of the State of Israel. The Palestinians could have had an independent Palestinian state in 1948 had they accepted the UN resolution instead of calling on the Arab countries to start a war against Israel. As for Israel, the United Nations took the right decision at the right time and did the Jewish people and the State of Israel a good service at a very crucial moment. In later years, the United Nations became quite unfriendly to Israel, due in large part to the structure of the organization.

The UN operates through regional groups. A majority of the UN's 183 members—108 states—are members in the Non-Aligned Group. Fifty-four of these 108 are Muslim countries, nearly half of which are Arab states. Therefore, it is almost automatic that any Arab resolution will pass in the General Assembly.

There were some incidents recently where some very influential Arab countries could not rally the support of the Muslim group and the Non-Aligned Group, and they failed in their attempt to bring to the Security Council some anti-Israeli resolutions. This happened during the debate over the deportees and the situation concerning the closure of the territories.

Being a country that does not belong to any formal geographical-political group makes it very hard for Israel to successfully operate at the UN. It also prevents Israel from becoming a legitimate and normal member of the United Nations, to have the right to be elected to positions, and to fully participate in the organization. Our natural place, of course, is the Asian group. When we will achieve peace with our Arab neighbors and the Palestinians, and I say when, not if, because I believe we will achieve peace with our Arab neighbors, then we will be able to be a member of the Asian group. But as long as this is not possible, we have to be part of some other regional group, so we can normalize our relationships with the organization and be able to participate in agencies and forums such as the Security Council, the Economic and Social Council, and so on.

We've been trying to resolve this matter for a very long time. Recently, I met with Douglas Bennet, the new Assistant Secretary of State for International Organizations, and with Madeleine Albright, the U.S. Ambassador to the UN. I also met all the ambassadors of the Western European and Others (W.E.O.) group. It is because of the positions of Britain and France that we cannot join the W.E.O. This is not because they are against us, but rather because they are afraid to open the door to others, such as the Baltic states. They are not so eager to share with others the very limited elected posts they now enjoy. Since acceptance to the W.E.O. is by consensus, it is not enough that we enjoy the support of all the other members of W.E.O.

Israel's Minister of Foreign Affairs met some ten days ago in Vienna with his British counterpart who promised him that Britain will not oppose our request for membership if there will be a consensus within the group. So this leaves us with France. Next week,

I will be meeting with the ambassador of France to the UN to discuss this matter, but of course the decision will be made by the French government.

We have three very supportive ambassadors on this matter: the United States, Belgian, and Canadian. Other countries, such as Denmark, Sweden, and Spain, will support us eventually. France holds the key, and if it announces that it will not oppose our request, then we have a good chance of becoming a member of W.E.O. soon. This will mark a breakthrough in our relations with the UN.

****

The new Israeli government takes a different approach to the UN than its predecessors. We do not see the United Nations as an anti-Semitic organization, and we do not feel that we are being persecuted by the member states. We see the United Nations, as do most countries, as a challenge, as an arena to influence international affairs. We would like to participate in any United Nations activities to normalize Israeli relations with all member states and the UN agencies and organizations. We participate not only in Israel-related debates but in any fora in which we feel obliged to participate.

We've been offered the chance to send individual Israelis to the peacekeeping forces, and we have been asked to participate in the task force to enhance democracy in countries where it still struggles to gain solid footing.

In September, the forty-eighth General Assembly will try to pass some anti-Israeli resolutions that are still on the agenda, although they have no relevance to the political and diplomatic realities of today. It is a shameful practice of the United Nations which for years has carried those resolutions. We try to defer those resolutions if not to eliminate them. We have held consultations with the United States Mission, and we are very hopeful that we will be able to defer some of those resolutions.

The key to any progress in the United Nations and in the international arena, in general, is connected in a very direct way to the peace process and to the prospect of achieving peace with our neighboring Arab countries. Israel needs a peaceful environment to fulfill its potential. A peaceful environment would enable Israel to attract investment, to stop the Arab boycott, to attract tourism, to generate regional development and cooperation, and of course, to strengthen our position in the United Nations.

Excerpted from a speech delivered to the National Jewish Communal Relations Council on 27 June 1993.

Israel and the United Nations: A New Perspective

A Checkered Past

The relationship between Israel and the United Nations has known ups and downs over the years. The relationship began with General Assembly resolution 181, of 29 November 1947, which served as the international legal basis for the end of the British Mandate and the establishment of the State of Israel. Commonly known as the "Partition Plan," this resolution called for the establishment in British Mandatory Palestine of two states, one Jewish and one Arab.

The plan was opposed by the Arabs, who tried to prevent its implementation by attacking the fledgling State of Israel on the day of its establishment, 14 May 1948. As a result of the war and subsequent political developments, Resolution 181 was only partially realized before it became obsolete. Almost one year later, on 11 May 1949, Israel was accepted as a member state of the United Nations.

In one of the great paradoxes of our time, the Arab countries and Palestinians have, since the 1967 Six Day War, observed 29 November as "Palestine Day" at the UN. They have done this despite their own rejection of the General Assembly resolution that would have created two states in Mandatory Palestine.

Dr. Ralph Bunche, an assistant to the United Nations Secretary-General at the time, mediated armistice agreements between Israel and the Arab states during the first half of 1949. Since then, further UN attempts to negotiate an end to the armed conflict proved unsuccessful. Its failure to maintain tranquility in the region was dramatized by Egypt's expulsion of UNEF peacekeeping forces from Sinai in 1967, a move that contributed to the outbreak of the Six Day War.

Since 1967, the United Nations and many of its agencies have assumed a hostile stance toward Israel. The Arab states found that the structure and patterns of activity in the UN gave them broad freedom of action in all UN bodies, with the exception of the Security Council. As a unified group with twenty members, and as members of the Asian group and African group, the Non-Aligned States, Group of 77, and Organization of the Islamic Conference, the Arabs have been able to mobilize a large bloc of states to support their agenda. Because there are over one hundred states in the Non-Aligned Group alone, the Arab and Moslem countries have often found majorities easy to obtain in the General Assembly.

Relentless attacks on Israel in all UN bodies assumed the character of a campaign to delegitimize the Jewish people's right to self-determination in an independent state. The campaign grew in intensity throughout the 1970s and reached its bitterest point on 10 November 1975 with the adoption of General Assembly Resolution 3379, which slandered Zionism as a form of racism and racial discrimination.

Until the present General Assembly, more than thirty anti-Israel resolutions have been adopted annually. In 1982, the Arabs began what became a yearly ritual and tried to block acceptance of Israel's credentials in an effort to prevent Israeli participation in the General Assembly. Because of procedural moves designed to quash the Arab initiative, the United Nations has functioned for the past three years without authorizing the credentials of any of its member states.

Despite this history of antagonism, the Security Council adopted Resolutions 242 (22 November 1967) and 338 (22 October 1973), which have constituted important foundations of all subsequent negotiations in the Middle East peace process. These resolutions were the first to incorporate the principles of peace, security, mutual recognition, and negotiation.

Toward a New Era

The dramatic changes in the geopolitical arena and in the Middle East have opened new opportunities for the Israel-UN relationship. The first major sign of this change came on 16 December 1991, after the convening of the Madrid Peace Conference on 30 October, when the General Assembly repealed resolution 3379 equating Zionism with racism.

Upon my appointment as ambassador to the United Nations in October 1992, I outlined four broad goals.

1. Change in the UN stance toward Israel.
2. Maximized Cooperation with all interested parties.
3. Increased Involvement and Participation in UN activities.
4. Normalization of Israel's relationship with the United Nations executive branch and member states.

With the changes in the world and the region, coupled with the new policies of the Rabin government and the agreements with the PLO and Jordan, these goals are steadily being met.

Change in UN Stance

General Assembly Resolutions

The forty-eighth General Assembly was a turning point in the Assembly's stance toward Israel and the Middle East.

A new resolution on the Middle East peace process was adopted, unprecedented in its positive character and constructive support for the achievements of the current peace process. In addition, of the approximately thirty negative resolutions raised annually, twenty-one were either not introduced, not brought to a vote, or changed in tone and content, with criticism and condemnation of Israel removed. The voting pattern in many cases also shifted in Israel's favor.

The resolutions of the forty-eighth General Assembly will be examined at length in the following pages.

Maximized Cooperation

Diplomatic Relations

The change in Israel's position at the UN has also found expression in the number of states with which Israel has diplomatic relations. Since the signing of the agreement with the PLO, relations with twelve states were established, seven of these signed at the UN.

The total number of states with which Israel has relations rose from 95 in 1990 to 138 this year. Of these, 133 are member states of the United Nations, whose total membership numbers 184.

UN Agencies

Israel and UN peacekeeping forces in the region (UNIFIL and UNDOF) maintained good relations, In addition, relations with UN agencies functioning in Israel and the territories (UNRWA, UNDP, and UNICEF) continued to improve. A level of coordination and cooperation that did not exist in the past has been reached.

Total investment by these agencies in the territories will grow from $300 million last year to almost $450 million in 1994. UNDP alone will double its allotment to the territories from $18 million to $40 million.

Increased Involvement and Participation

Committee on Information

Israel's acceptance by consensus to the Committee on Information marks the first time that Israel was appointed to a permanent committee of the UN.

Election of an Israeli to UN Administrative Tribunal

Former director of the Justice Ministry Mayer Gabay was elected to the UN Administrative Tribunal in direct elections by secret ballot. This marks the first time since the early 1960s that an Israeli was elected to serve on a UN body.

Other Issues

Israel addressed many issues at the forty-eighth General Assembly beyond those related directly to the Middle East. Israeli representatives spoke on sustainable development, environment and desertification, women's rights, democracy, drugs, apartheid, human rights, and other issues.

Normalization

Credentials

For the first time in twelve years, the credentials of all member states, including Israel, were accepted without hindrance.

General Atmosphere

The changed political atmosphere was reflected in other ways as well.

The Secretary General and ambassadors of all the members of the Security Council with which Israel has diplomatic relations attended with their spouses a dinner in honor of Israeli Prime Minister Yitzhak Rabin, hosted by Mrs. Yaacobi and myself.

More than one hundred ambassadors and foreign ministers attended a reception for Israeli Foreign Minister Shimon Peres, held at the United Nations building during the General Assembly.

****

The change in the relationship between Israel and the United Nations, however, is not yet complete.

- Israel must join a geographic group at the UN. Its natural place is with the Asian group, yet political realities still make this impossible. Until then, Israel should be accepted as a member of the Western European and Others group.
- The number of Israelis elected and appointed to UN bodies should be increased, as should Israeli involvement in UN peacekeeping efforts.
- Israel would like to broaden cooperation at the United Nations with all states, both those that have established formal relations and those that have not.
- Israel also wants to broaden its cooperation with UN agencies and executive bodies.
- Greater changes in UN resolutions must be effected to make them reflective of and appropriate to the new reality in the Middle East.
- Israel will continue to increase its involvement at the United Nations in issues not directly related to the Middle East and Israel.

The United Nations is not an inherently hostile organization with regard to Israel. Rather, it is a forum in which Israel should participate as a full and equal member. In 1993, the United Nations made significant progress in bringing its resolutions into tune with the new reality in the Middle East. Still, much work needs to be done. The deferral and discontinuation of several obsolete resolutions and the changes in language and content of many others will serve as precedents as the UN continues to adapt to the new situation in the region.

Excerpted from a summary of the forty-eighth UN General Assembly, 11 January 1994.

At Last, Part of the UN Club

For years, when it came to the Middle East, the UN was used as a battleground for political warfare against Israel. But since the end of the Cold War, the United Nation's role in world affairs has expanded, and Western leaders have called upon the organization to redefine its priorities, goals and methods. President Bill Clinton, in his address to the General Assembly last October, captured the sentiment when he said it was time to "reinvent how the United Nations operates." That process has in fact begun. And breakthroughs in the Mideast peace process are forcing the United Nations to reinvent its stance toward Israel and the Arab-Israeli conflict as well.

Even the Hebron massacre did not change the new realities at the United Nations. We maintained contacts withe the PLO observer and the Egyptian ambassador throughout the crisis; and when the Security Council adopted its resolution, it condemned the massacre—not Israel. The resolution included strong words, but the vicious anti-Israel language of the past was not there.

Looking further back, positive changes occurred last year in General Assembly resolutions on Middle East issues, in Israel's work with UN agencies, and in Israel's bilateral relations with other member states. The improvement was especially evident in the recent General Assembly, which began shortly after the signing of the Israel-PLO Declaration of Principles. The session began with three important developments: For the first time since 1981, Israel's credentials were accepted without opposition. For the first time, since the early '60s, an Israeli was chosen to serve on a UN body, with Mayer Gabay's election to the UN Administrative Tribunal. And for the first time ever, Israel was appointed to a UN permanent committee, the Committee on Information.

The real turning point came in the General Assembly resolutions on the Middle East. First, the Assembly adopted a new resolution supporting the Mideast peace process. Conceived by Israel and introduced by the United States, Russia and Norway, it was cosponsored by 110 countries and supported by 155. Only Syria, Lebanon, and Iran opposed it, Libya abstained, and Iraq was absent.

Furthermore, of the approximately thirty anti-Israel resolutions raised annually in the past, twenty-one either were not introduced, were not brought to a vote, or were changed, with criticism and condemnation of Israel removed. During the entire process, we were in direct consultation with the Egyptian ambassador and the PLO observer, who acted as intermediaries for the Arab group as a whole.

We were pleased to note that even with the moderation of some of these resolutions, support for them began to crumble. In 1992, for instance, a resolution on "Israeli nuclear armament" passed by sixty-four to three, with ninety abstentions. The 1993 resolution was toned down, so that it no longer "deplores Israeli refusal to renounce possession of nuclear weapons." Even so, it passed only by fifty-three to forty-five. The shift in voting patterns could lead to the removal of many such resolutions from next year's agenda.

Israel also continued to improve relations with UN peacekeeping forces in the region and UN agencies functioning in the territories. Budgets allocated to social and economic development in the territories will grow from $300 million last year to almost $450 million in 1994. The UN Development Project alone will more than double its allotment to the territories from $18 million to $40 million. This aid is vital to creating economic conditions conducive to implementing the accord with the PLO.

With the change in Israel's position, the UN is providing a comfortable forum for developing bilateral relations with other countries. Since the signing of the agreement with the PLO, ties have been established or renewed with fifteen states; seven of the agreements creating ties were signed at the UN. We are broadening contact with other countries, including Arab and Muslim ones, and proceeding with discussions to establish ties with more countries.

We also continue to increase our involvement at the United Nations in issues not directly related to the Mideast and Israel. In this regard, we would like to see more Israelis elected and appointed to UN bodies and peacekeeping operations as an expression of the UN's willingness to open its doors to Israeli professionals.

The turning point in 1993 was a direct result of the new political climate in our region and in the world. Further advancement toward peace in the Middle East will ensure the continued improvement of UN-Israel relations.

Article originally published in *The Jerusalem Report* 5 May 1994.

The World Has Been Opened for Israel

Even if the danger of Islamic fundamentalist terrorism and the weakness of the Palestinian Authority continue, the Middle East will not revert to the *status quo ante,* and the changes that have taken place in the past year will be lasting ones.

The peace treaty with Jordan, the change in Israeli-Palestinian relations, and the deepening ties with Arab and Muslim countries are dramatic turning points, offering new possibilities to us.

The world is opening up for Israel. This is felt not only through investment, tourism, and reciprocal relations in the fields of science and culture. The new openness also finds expression in the positions of the international community and in our expanding relations with other states.

I have never believed in the paranoid, isolationist sentiment that "The whole world is against us." On 29 November 1947, the United Nations decided on the establishment of the State of Israel and an Arab state next to it. The United States, many countries in Europe, South America, Oceania and Asia proved themselves to be, and remained throughout the years, friends of Israel, despite the differences of opinion that are a normal part of any relationship.

Lately, Israel has become more and more of a partner, participant, catalyst, and influence in the international system, via its relations with the countries that compose it.

Twenty-seven states have established or renewed relations with Israel in the past year and a half. Of the 184 United Nations member states, 149 have diplomatic relations with Israel. The Security Council has condemned terrorist attacks in Israel directed against Israelis. Israeli candidates have been elected to UN posts by secret ballot in the General Assembly. Israel also has begun to participate in UN peacekeeping operations.

Ambassadors from a number of Arab and Muslim countries maintain regular professional contact with us. The majority of anti–Israel resolutions have been deleted or changed. Our voice is heard and many times even sought.

Of course, there are still divisions and disagreements in a number of areas, principally in those regarding the permanent status arrangements to be worked out in the peace process: Jerusalem, borders, arms control and oversight regimes, and so forth. But there is no longer a debate about legitimacy or about the right to exist or about Israel's participation in the regional and international community.

The world is ready and waiting, and it is up to us to integrate ourselves, to make our voice heard, to have a say in what happens, and to promote our interests in such fields as economics, science, and culture.

This is happening in Casablanca, in the multilateral negotiations, in the arrangements for cooperation with the European Union. It is happening in the UN agencies for development and assistance, and in direct talks, some open, others secret, with various countries and with other actors in the international community.

The world is opening up. Our job is to see the new opportunities as they arise and to actively make the most of the new, positive environment.

Unpublished article written 31 October 1994.

Commemoration of the Fiftieth Anniversary of the United Nations

Almost fifty years ago, the framers of the Charter of the United Nations set great challenges by making a far-reaching commitment to the loftiest ideals of humankind. "To strengthen universal peace. . . . to achieve international cooperation in solving international problems . . . and in encouraging respect for human rights and fundamental freedoms. . . . [and] to be a centre for harmonizing the actions of nations in the attainment of these common ends."

As we review the past five decades, we can take pride in the UN's impressive accomplishments and progress toward meeting these ideals. Yet we can see that the great task has just begun.

It is an unfortunate fact that only a minority of countries currently enjoy truly democratic systems. While democratization cannot be imposed from the outside, the UN can and should promote education toward democracy. Not only is democracy essential for human rights to be fully respected, but it is also a necessary condition for lasting peace, stability, and economic and social progress.

The United Nations should be especially sensitive to this truth, having been founded in the aftermath of World War II, on the ruins of a world laid waste by the forces of tyranny and fascism.

It is Israel's hope that the Middle East—in its search for peace, stability and prosperity—might become a model of hope for the entire international community. Despite many obstacles, we have recently seen in our region great progress toward a brighter future. This progress is based on direct, bilateral negotiations between parties who desire to replace conflict with cooperation.

The peace process began with a conference held in Madrid, cosponsored by the United States and the Russian Federation. It was followed by bilateral negotiations on several tracks and by multilateral talks and the Casablanca Conference that are enhancing regional cooperation to create a better economic and social reality for all peoples of the Middle East.

As the prospects for peace grow, there is a need to devote more resources to social and economic development in the region. The United Nations, through such agencies as UNDP, UNRWA, and UNICEF, has been contributing to meet the basic needs of the Palestinians in the West Bank and Gaza. Now, these and other agencies are making increased efforts in cooperation with Israel, the Palestinian Authority, and the donor countries to change the human, social, and economic realities in these areas. Such a change is a necessary basis for a changed state of mind, one marked by an unflagging commitment to peaceful coexistence. The United Nations' role in the Middle East during the next fifty years will necessarily be affected by these far-reaching changes.

Over the past five decades, the relationship between Israel and the United Nations has known both high and low points. The realities of Cold War politics created an automatic majority in the General Assembly that would support almost any initiative, no matter how outrageous, which was designed to single out Israel for condemnation. These moves tried to make Israel an outcast from the family of nations. It is our hope that this blemish on the record of the UN will remind all States of the dangers of abusing this forum of peace. By repealing in 1991 the resolution that libeled Zionism as a form of racism, the General Assembly took an important step in demonstrating that this lesson is being taken to heart.

Israel owes a noble debt to the United Nations. It was the UN that, on 29 November 1947, adopted a resolution that restored sovereignty to the Jewish people after two thousand years of exile from their land. Then on 11 May 1949, the General Assembly welcomed the new State of Israel as a member state of the United Nations.

Following the 1967 Six Day War, the Security Council adopted Resolution 242, which affirms the right of every state in the area "to live in peace within secure and recognized boundaries free from threats or acts of force." The Security Council reaffirmed this right in Resolution 338, adopted during the 1973 Yom Kippur War.

In the light of the historic steps toward peace in our region, Israel has encouraged the General Assembly to avoid adopting anachronistic resolutions detached from the new reality. We welcome the progress that has already been made—the adoption of Resolution 48/58, which welcomed the Middle East peace process and the agreements between Israel and the PLO and Israel and Jordan; the removal of contentious language and issues from other resolutions on the Middle East; and the elimination of obsolete resolutions that were contrary to the new reality. We look forward to further progress in this area, which would be a constructive expression of the United Nations' commitment to the Middle East peace process begun in Madrid.

Israel is pleased that its national preparations for the celebration of the fiftieth anniversary of the United Nations are taking place in an atmosphere of increasing cooperation and improved relations between Israel and the UN. Our commemoration, which will include the printing of a fiftieth anniversary postage stamp, and the convening of an international conference, will devote special attention to cultural and educational activities aimed at informing the Israeli public about the recent positive developments in Israel-UN relations, and calling for Israel's active participation in the UN system.

Israel looks forward to increased involvement in United Nations activities. Over the past year, Israel has participated in the civilian and humanitarian spheres in peacekeeping activities in Rwanda and Haiti, and in election-monitoring in South Africa and Mozambique and has contributed in other areas as well. For the first time in over thirty years, Israeli candidates were elected in direct and personal elections to serve in UN committees and bodies.

Unfortunately, Israel has been refused membership in a geographic group at the UN and is thus barred from membership in all UN bodies in which the elections are based on regional quotas of representation. As the UN enters a new stage in its existence, we again urge our fellow member states to rectify this grave breach of the principle of universality and to help ensure respect for the sovereign equality of all member states as envisioned in the Charter of the United Nations.

In ancient Israel, every fiftieth year was celebrated as a year of liberty and renewal. In Hebrew, it is called "yovel," from which derives the English word *jubilee*. As it is written in Leviticus, 25.9, "Then shalt thou cause the trumpet of the jubilee to sound. . . . And ye shall hallow the fiftieth year and proclaim liberty throughout all the land unto all the inhabitants thereof."

May the jubilee of the United Nations mark a year of renewal for the organization. May it be a year of peace and abundance, proclaiming liberty throughout all the world unto all the inhabitants thereof.

Excerpted from a speech delivered in the United Nations General Assembly, 9 November 1994.

Part Two
Toward Peace and Cooperation

3

Making Peace

Great Chance for Brave Decisions

PEACE talks between Israel and its Arab neighbors resume in Washington today, less than two weeks before the American presidential election.

At this juncture, it seems clear that any breakthrough in the negotiations may be unattainable without a summit meeting between Prime Minister Yitzhak Rabin and Syria's President Hafez Assad, under the sponsorship of the U.S. president.

It is worth recalling that negotiations between Israel and Egypt had been going on for a year and a half when President Jimmy Carter hosted the Israeli prime minister and Egyptian president at Camp David in 1978. As a result, the Camp David Accords, and subsequently the peace treaty between Israel and Egypt, were reached.

The bilateral peace talks and the multilateral negotiations have created a new dynamic, and prospects are good. A breakthrough toward a peace treaty between Israel and Syria would act as the catalyst for change in the entire Middle East. If it doesn't happen, the train will appear to have been halted at the first station, with all steam lost.

It is a near certainty that a Syrian-Israeli peace treaty would lead to an Israeli-Palestinian arrangement on autonomy. This would mean a real chance of achieving a peace agreement with Jordan, Lebanon, and perhaps Saudi Arabia as well.

The agreements should be based on full peace, diplomatic relations, unimpeded passage of trade and people, early warning and security arrangements, and an end to acts of hostility. They also should be based on Security Council Resolution 242, that calls for an Israeli concession on territories (not "the territories").

Regarding the Golan Heights, it should be noted that Arabs do not live there, and owing to topographical and strategic conditions, the Golan is in part, a vital defense and early-warning factor for Israel. But the government of Israel holds that Resolution 242 does not apply to the Golan.

Many Israelis are disturbed by the nature of the regimes in Syria, Jordan, Lebanon, and Saudi Arabia. These are not democracies, reliant upon checks and balances, a change of regime might cause a radical change in policy.

Democratization in the Arab countries, and indeed throughout the world, is more than a political and moral issue; it is directly tied to the existence of peace and stability. In the absence of democracy in the Arab countries. Israel should ensure an effective security and deterrent policy in the progress toward peace.

An encouraging, even revolutionary, development in the history of the nations of the Middle East is a growing awareness that peace, economic development, and the general well-being of people in the region are all interdependent.

Since the Arab states' violation of the UN's resolutions and their attack on Israel immediately upon the founding of the state in 1948, the continuing conflict has exacted a tremendous price from the nations of the region. The direct cost of the wars and the indirect cost of defense, along with closed borders and the lack of trade ties and tourism, have been major factors in halting economic and human development.

Nevertheless, Israel, despite being the object of aggression, isolation, and hostility, has developed appreciably. Its Jewish population has quintupled since 1948, the per-capita standard of living has risen sixfold, and exports are now forty times the 1950 rate. But the Arab-Israeli wars alone have cost the economy $40 billion, while the cost of the Arab boycott has been almost $20 billion. The lack of free flow of people, goods, and services has exacted a very heavy price.

Political unreadiness and short-sightedness have littered the history of the Middle East with wasted opportunities for a breakthrough to peace, at a tragic price. Hopefully, the lesson has been learned and great opportunities will bring about great and courageous decisions.

Only when the guns fall silent and the peoples of the region can devote themselves to improving their quality of life rather than to military confrontation and futile hatred, will the Middle East once again become a model civilization. At stake are the lives and well-being of hundreds of millions of people and the future of us all.

Article originally published in The Jerusalem Post 21 October 1992.

Mideast Peace Talks Must Not Be Derailed

William Safire is partially correct when he asserts in "Eight Rounds to Go" (column, 19 Nov.) that time is not on the Arab side and that President Hafez al-Assad of Syria will "never get back on the Golan if he loses Rabin." However, this is more than a political power game. The people of Syria, Israel, and the entire Middle East will lose if the peace negotiations should fail. The Middle East is the land of missed opportunities for peace, and all of us have paid a painful price. Peace itself is the best kind of security if it is based on security arrangements, open borders, and full normalization.

Mr. Safire writes that "this is the moment to discover whether direct negotiation between Arabs and Jews has a future." Direct negotiations between Israel and its Arab neighbors are the best and most natural way to achieve peace, but if direct negotiations do not succeed, the stakes are too high to allow the process to fail.

Sometimes, negotiations are reminiscent of the humorous saying, What is the difference between a monologue and a dialogue? A monologue is when one person talks to himself. A dialogue is when two people talk to themselves. In 1974, separation of forces agreements were reached among Syria, Egypt, and Israel through the mediation of Henry Kissinger, and so was the interim agreement in 1975 between Israel and Egypt.

Direct negotiations are no doubt preferable to third-party mediation. However, if the alternative is failure, then assistance will be necessary. We cannot allow the alternative to peace to occur.

Published letter to the editor of the *New York Times* written 20 November 1992.

Question of Palestine: United Nations 1992

Nineteen years ago today, Mr. David Ben-Gurion, the founding father of the State of Israel, passed away. It is only fitting, then, that I commence by quoting his prophetic words, spoken in 1960, regarding this organization:

> a form of higher moral rule is being formed which tries to safeguard world peace and peace among nations which are bound one to another . . . it is most likely that the United Nations will have a role to play in drawing men together and establishing peace among nations.

I would like to propose to our Palestinian neighbors in the territories that we leave behind the syndromes of the past. Together, let us do our utmost to reach an agreement as soon as possible on self-governing administrative autonomy, based on the Camp David Accords and the letter of invitation to the Madrid Peace Conference and the proposals put forward by the government of Israel. Let us not allow radical groups to drag us down the path of confrontation and bloodshed. Bitter emotions and fanaticism should be pushed aside, so we may all embark responsibly on the road of humanism and peace.

If we focus our efforts on the positive path toward reconciliation and peace, then the State of Israel, the Arab states, and the Palestinians will all benefit from it. It will enhance our well-being and safeguard our security, and it will serve future generations by improving the quality of life.

The confidence-building measures initiated thus far by the new Israeli government aim to create a new political and human environment in the region. They aim to improve the ability to conduct a constructive dialogue between the Palestinians and Israel. These concrete steps are designed to defuse tensions and increase mutual confidence and trust.

I hope that the peace process will bring an end to violence. Violence only brings about more violence, whether it harms Arabs, Jews, or others.

We will need to reach a political settlement in stages. The first stage will be autonomy. In the course of the bilateral peace talks in Washington, which are under the cosponsorship of the United States and the Russian Federation, Israel has proposed the concept of a Palestinian Administrative Council (PAC). This elected body would, under the interim self-government arrangement (ISGA) agreements, assume broad powers and responsibilities in order to deal with the vast majority of the Palestinians' day-to-day affairs. These responsibilities would extend to aspects of infrastructure such as land use and water, as will be determined in the ISGA agreement.

The Israeli proposals envision democratic elections to the administrative council. The council members would be accountable to their electorate and would discharge their designated functions in the framework of the ISGA agreement. Such elections would be unprecedented for the Palestinians, and the modalities would be based on the preservation of the right of free assembly, free expression, and secret ballots.

Israel has suggested that the PAC administer the following fifteen spheres of operation:

Under the ISGA agreement, the administrative council, as an administrative-functional body, would wield general executive powers within its spheres of operation, including the power to promulgate regulations and bylaws, and to exercise general executive functions.

The negotiations between Israel and the joint Jordanian-Palestinian delegation regarding the permanent status of the territories are meant to begin in the third year of the interim self-government arrangements. This phase of the negotiations will be carried out on the basis of Security Council Resolutions 242 and 338, as established in the ground rules of the Madrid process. In this second phase, the permanent status issues of territory, security, and peace will be addressed.

If all our energy will be channeled to a positive direction, then we could work toward improving education, health, agriculture, infrastructure, employment, and the quality of life of all the people of the region.

The bilateral peace negotiations are due to resume in Washington in just six days, on 7 December 1992. On this occasion, I call upon the Palestinian delegation to the peace talks to play an active and positive role in the negotiations. Do not turn away the great opportunity this has developed for both of us.

Let us depart from the obsolete and anachronistic attitudes and resolutions of the past. Those resolutions are not relevant to today, when peace negotiations are in progress. Let us depart from the notion of the status quo, which proved to be a dangerous illusion, in light of the very bitter and painful experiences in our past. The only way to avoid another painful experience for all of us is to detach ourselves from emotionally satisfying demagoguery and to divert all of our efforts to the negotiating table and toward reconciliation and peace.

Excerpted from a speech delivered in the United Nations General Assembly, 1 December 1992.

On Tolerance

The principal commitment of the international community to tolerance was enshrined in the preamble of the United Nations Charter. The Member States committed themselves to "practice tolerance and live together in peace with one another as good neighbors." The founders of this body understood that only through encouraging tolerance among the peoples of the world could the scourge of war be eliminated. Only thus could the world hope to survive and progress.

We come from different parts of the world. We differ in color, in culture, in religion. We have different beliefs and opinions, but all of us are human beings.

Judaism places the notion of tolerance and respect for others as one of its highest ideals. Rabbi Akiva, the great Jewish sage, was once approached by a non-Jew who wished to convert to Judaism. "The only thing you must learn," said the wise rabbi, "do not unto your fellow what is hateful to yourself!"

Judaism has always encouraged discussion and disagreement, but within bounds of tolerance. Indeed, our entire oral law, the Talmud, is based on the discourse between two schools of thought—Beit Hillel and Beit Shamai. The debates between the two schools, no matter how heated, were confined to the realm of discussion. Thus, the murderer of Yitzhak Rabin acted in complete contravention to the morals and principals of Judaism. He removed himself from the entire Jewish people.

Our history is full of tragic examples of mistreatment at the hands of others. We felt the pain of intolerance and we learned its bitter lessons.

Prejudice against Jews reached its climax in the first half of this century. In the 1930s, the Nazis of Germany came to power espousing a racist ideology based on the superiority of one group over another. Jews, along with several other groups, were singled out by the Nazis for annihilation. Between 1939–45, six million Jews were exterminated by the Nazis for the sole crime of being born Jewish.

The return of the Jewish people to its homeland in Israel was based on the idea of creating a moral and just society where equality and mutual respect would prevail. In its Declaration of Independence, the State of Israel promised to "uphold the full social and political equality of all of its citizens, without distinction of race, creed or sex."

To our detriment, our region has known many years of hatred and war. Israel has fought for many years in order to achieve a lasting and equitable peace with its neighbors based on co-existence and mutual respect.

During the last three years we have witnessed a dramatic change in the prospects for peace in the Middle East. Our goal is to transform the agreements which are being forged on the ground today into real cooperation and neighborly relations tomorrow.

Sadly, the progress achieved between Israel and its neighbors during the last several years has been ignored by some in our region. There are still those who refuse to accept the new reality. There are radicals and extremists on both sides. There are those who place bombs on buses or who attempt through murder and other inhumane actions to stop the due process for peace. These people are out of touch with the new reality. They represent a fanatic approach of hatred and political myopia.

As recent events in the Middle East have proven, it is a slippery slope from angry rhetoric to violent actions. Dehumanizing a nation or a group of people based on their beliefs or worldview cannot be reconciled with any definition of tolerance. The world has witnessed these phenomena too many times during the twentieth century. The international community must be aware that violent rhetoric often leads to violent actions. We must accept the responsibility to keep disputes within democratic tolerance.

During this violent century, some of the world's greatest leaders have been brutally taken from us by the enemies of peace and progress. Mahatma Gandhi, Anwar al-Sadat, Martin Luther King, Jr. and John F. Kennedy were all snuffed out by assassins' bullets.

It was mentioned already that two weeks ago, to our great sorrow, this happened in Israel. The murder of Prime Minister Rabin was an act of fanatics; of fundamentalists; of radicals. The murderer stands outside the scope of Judaism, universal morality, and democratic tolerance. He murdered a great statesman; a courageous warrior for peace; a man of great integrity and devotion. Yitzhak Rabin will be missed not only by Israel and the entire Jewish people, but by peoples throughout the Middle East and the whole world. His path for peace and reconciliation will be continued. His vision will be fulfilled.

There is no coming to terms with what has happened. We can only fight against it by educating our children; by raising our voices in protest; by refusing to surrender to hatred and intolerance and by enhancing peace.

The Year of Tolerance has come to an end, but the need for tolerance has not. The international community must remain committed not to the notion of tolerance, but to its attainment on a day-to-day basis.

Excerpted from a speech delivered at the United Nations General Assembly, 20 November 1995.

Peace for the Middle East and Israel

A week ago, we hopefully closed the file at the United Nations Security Council on the issue of the temporary removal of Hamas and Islamic Jihad terrorists. This was achieved following the agreement between Israel and the United States that was concluded by Prime Minister Yitzhak Rabin and Secretary of State Warren Christopher. As I told the President of the Security Council, the Moroccan Ambassador to the United Nations Mr. Ahmed Snoussi, last Friday, "I hope that we all can concentrate on the most important goal, which is the renewal of the peace talks between Israel and its neighbors."

The measures taken by Israel against the Islamic fundamentalist terrorists of Hamas and Islamic Jihad were acts of self-defense. Islamic fundamentalists, who are supported, financed, and backed by Iran, are casting a shadow over the entire Middle East. From Iran to the Sudan, from Jordan to Algeria, in Egypt and in the territories, fundamentalists have an increasing amount of influence. They are obtaining it either through ballots or through bullets.

The other matter that the ongoing dialogue between the United States and Israel is dealing with is the mutual effort to revive the peace talks.

This is the most significant challenge for Israel and for the countries of the region: to make a breakthrough toward peace and reconciliation. This is perhaps a one-time opportunity, and we must grab it before it slips away.

I believe that following the trip of the Secretary of State to the Middle East, all the parties to the negotiations will come back to the negotiating table in April. I believe that it is an irreversible process and I hope Syria, Lebanon, Jordan, and the Palestinians will not miss this opportunity. There is no alternative to peace anywhere, particularly not in the Middle East. Israel is fully committed to doing our utmost to achieve peace.

The world is changing very rapidly. Five years ago, the historian Francis Fukuyama wrote in a very decisive manner that history has ended. But history is alive and kicking—that is, the collapse of the Soviet Union, the end of the Cold War, regional economic unification (EEC, 1 January 1993), the rise of ethnic conflicts, and international intervention.

We are facing a new era worldwide and in the Middle East as well. Just imagine if one had been asked four years ago what would happen in the next four years. I dare say that no one would have predicted the disintegration of the Soviet Union, the Gulf War, the Middle East peace process, the massive aliyah from the USSR, the dramatic cut in long-range missiles, and many other developments that have occurred during the past four years.

But even if, since the end of the Cold War, the threat of a nuclear war has lessened, the world has not become a safer place. Since World War II, there have been 110 wars that have left at least twenty-five million people dead. Presently, there are forty-eight active ethnic, religious and national conflicts raging across the globe,—some of them with explosive potential.

The changing of the guard, of the governments, in the United States and in Israel, is a change of agenda, which means for Israel a change in the scale of priorities:

- achieving peace and security, instead of the Greater Israel approach;
- absorption of aliyah, instead of establishing new settlements in the territories;
- maintaining Israel as a democratic state and the homeland of the Jewish people, instead of annexation.

But still too many states in the region are putting their resources, their human energies, and their creativity to waste by continuing to pursue conflict. If all those resources would instead be devoted to investment in human capital and economic development, we could be improving lives rather than ending them. If we invest in health, education, and science instead of military hardware, then the Middle East could one day be free from hunger and illiteracy.

This is the right place and the right audience to remind everyone that only once was a peace treaty achieved between Israel and an Arab state, Egypt. When I met with former President Jimmy Carter today, I told him that this was a historic step, and that Israel, Egypt, and the entire region would not forget his contribution to it. Since then, Egypt has reduced its armed forces by half, and there have not been any military conflicts between us. A cold peace is better than a hot war.

An important and encouraging development is the growing awareness of the interdependence between peace, economic development, and the general well-being of people in the region.

The cost of the ongoing situation has been too high for all of us. Consider the burden and cost of war and hostility, the arms race, and the lost opportunities for economic growth, trade, and development of regional infrastructures. The potential fruits of peace are immense, such as a reduction in the cost of defense and in arms procurement, open borders, trade and tourism, and investment in educational, health, and scientific development. Instead of exchanging insults and bullets, the people of the Middle East could be exchanging technology and know-how. Instead of investing in the weapons of war, we could be enjoying together the prosperity of peace.

Peace is not just the best form of security—it touches upon the substance of Israel's existence. To be or nor to be is not the question any more but rather what to be and how to be:

- a state of the Jewish people;
- a democratic state;
- a nation of excellence with a high quality of life;
- a society and economy that absorbs massive immigration and provides young Israelis with a proper opportunity for studying, for employment, and for creativity.

Some progress has already been made in the peace talks between Israel and its Arab neighbors, but still we have a long way to go.

- Jordan: A mutual working agenda was signed.

We believe that the differences can be bridged.

- Syria: The negotiations are focusing on the real issues—security, peace, and borders (territory).

The Prime Minister has stated that Israel is ready for a partial withdrawal *on* the Golan Heights in the framework of a full peace treaty

- *the Palestinians:* It is the first time serious negotiations are being conducted, on the basis of the Camp David Accords and new Israeli proposals.

Namely, to establish self-government administrative autonomy as an interim stage for three to five years, until the negotiations resume concerning the final settlement.

Speech to the Southern Center for International Studies, Atlanta, Georgia, 18 February 1993.

An Open Letter to a Palestinian Friend

As both an Israeli and as your neighbor, allow me to speak to you personally.

I was born in 1935 in the Land of Israel, which at the time was called Palestine. My parents were among the founders of the first moshav, a cooperative village, in the Hefer Valley between Tel Aviv and Haifa.

Next to the village where I was born and grew up, there were some Arab villages. I met their boys in the fields, we washed together in the same stream and a number of them were my friends.

On 29 November 1947, the General Assembly of the United Nations decided upon the establishment of two states in the Land of Israel: the State of Israel and an Arab (Palestinian) state. Israel accepted the decision of the Assembly, but the Palestinians and the Arab states rejected it and launched a massive armed invasion in order to eradicate Israel. Although there were just 650,000 Jews living in Israel, we emerged victorious, though we paid a heavy price in casualties.

As a result of the war, Jordan occupied the West Bank and Egypt occupied the Gaza Strip. During the nineteen years Jordan controlled those areas, it did not set up a Palestinian state. In 1967, when Israel was again threatened with destruction by its neighboring Arab states, the territories came under our control, along with the Golan Heights, in a war of self-defense.

We are aware of the suffering that the Palestinians have experienced throughout this long period. But it is not Israel that has refused to sign a peace treaty since 1947.

There is now a government in Israel that does not desire the annexation of the territories and that seeks to move forward toward peace. I would like to tell you with all sincerity that it is not a search for a solution to the Palestinian problem that guides us, but rather a solution to the Israeli problem. We do not desire to rule nearly two million Palestinians against their will and to turn Israel into a binational state, nor do we wish to have a nondemocratic state.

But Israel does seek appropriate security arrangements, in light of the bitter lessons of the past, and to guarantee the existence of a united Jerusalem, the capital of Israel.

I propose to you, our Palestinian neighbors, that we leave behind the syndromes of the past. Let us do our utmost to reach an agreement. Let us not allow radical groups to drag us down the path of confrontation and bloodshed. Violence only brings about more violence. Bitter emotions and fanaticism should be pushed aside, so we can all embark responsibly on the road to peace.

If we would focus our efforts on the positive path toward reconciliation and peace, then all would benefit from it. It would enhance our well-being and safeguard our security. Peace would bring an end to violence.

We need to reach a political settlement in stages. The first stage is autonomy. In the course of the bilateral peace talks in Washington, which are under the cosponsorship of the United States and the Russian Federation, Israel has proposed the concept of a Palestinian Administrative Council. This elected body would, under the interim self-government arrangement agreements, assume broad powers and responsibilities in order to deal with the vast majority of the Palestinians' day-to-day affairs in the areas of agriculture, health, education, finance and budgets, labor, police, tourism, transportation and communications, municipal affairs, and so forth.

The negotiations between Israel and the Palestinians regarding the permanent status of the territories are meant to begin in the third year of the interim self-government arrangements. This phase of the negotiations would be carried out on the basis of Security Council Resolutions 242 and 338. In this second phase, the permanent status issues of territory, security, and peace would be addressed.

Achieving an agreement between us, the Palestinians, and Israel would, I believe, bring about a peace agreement with Jordan and eventually with Syria and Lebanon as well.

Let us depart from the notion of the status quo, which proved to be a dangerous illusion. The only way to avoid another painful experience is to divert all our efforts to the negotiation table and toward reconciliation. Now is a one time opportunity to achieve peace. Let us make sure that we do not allow it to slip away.

Article originally published in *The Jewish Week,* 9–15 July 1993.

Time for Bold Steps

I am very happy to be here with all of you tonight. These are, I believe, great days for Israel, for the peoples of the Middle East, as well as for the United States and the other democratic countries. I also believe these are great days for the Jewish people as a whole.

We now live in a new era; an era of rapid change. It is not the "new world order" that was predicted by some. Rather, it is a "new world disorder." Instead of a bipolar world, we now have, following the collapse of the Soviet Union, a multipolar world.

Instead of capitalist-communist tension, we have ethnic, religious, and national unrest around the world.

As a result of such changes we are witnessing a new era in the Middle East. For Israel, this new era has opened up new opportunities.

For the first time in the history of the Middle East, direct peace talks are being conducted between Israel, her neighboring Arab countries and the Palestinians. Yes, we are facing difficulties and hardships, but I believe this is an irreversible process.

We are witnessing now a historical change: an agreement between Israel and the Palestinians. It may end a hundred years of hostility and bloodshed. At last, it seems that the Palestinians are ready to acknowledge the simple reality that Israel is an existing, strong, and developing neighbor state and that we must live in peace.

Although this new Israeli-Palestinian agreement has certain novel aspects, many of the principles are not new at all. They can be found in the Camp David Accords in which the two-step approach remains the basis for the process. According to the Camp David Accords, Palestinians were to be granted self-governing autonomy for five years. A permanent settlement based on UN Security Council Resolutions 242 and 338 was to be implemented after two years of autonomy. Even the decision to allow elections in the territories is not a new one, it was first made in 1989 during the time of the Israeli National Unity Government, made up of both the Likud and Labor parties.

Ever since the Madrid Conference, Israel has negotiated with Palestinians from the Territories. As every Israeli and Arab child knows, these Palestinians received their instructions directly from PLO headquarters in Tunis.

It is true that the Camp David Accords, signed by the late Menachem Begin, did not include an early implementation of a self-governing authority in Gaza and Jericho as the current Declaration of Principles does, but it is also true that the Camp David Accords left the status of Jerusalem during the planned period of autonomy open. The current Declaration of Principles does not. It clearly states that the status of Jerusalem will only be discussed as part of the negotiations for a permanent settlement. A settlement that will be implemented after five years of autonomous rule. Israel has already made it clear: Jerusalem will stay undivided under Israeli sovereignty. The Declaration of Principles also grants that Israel will retain responsibilities for Israeli citizens and other aspects of security in the territories for the five years of autonomy. The Camp

David Accords did not guarantee that. Furthermore, for peace with Egypt, Begin's government gave up the entire Sinai Peninsula. Rabin's government has designed a step-by-step mechanism for peace with the Palestinians.

Historic opportunities, such as the one materializing right now, are very rare and are made from a combination of circumstance and personalities. In 1948, the State of Israel was born because of the world's guilt over the Holocaust, the fall of the British Empire, and the leadership of David Ben-Gurion. In 1978, the Camp David Accords were made possible through the leadership of President Sadat of Egypt, the support of President Jimmy Carter, the joint leadership of Menachem Begin, Moshe Dayan, and Ezer Weitzman, and the commitment to peace by the Labor Party.

Today's historic opportunity has materialized because the growth of Islamic fundamentalism as a violent threat to all moderates and world stability, the disintegration of the Soviet Union and with it, the turning around of the new Russian Federation to support the peace process; and a moderate government in Israel that combines Yitzhak Rabin's unquestionable authority on matters of national security and the diplomatic skills and creativity of Foreign Minister Shimon Peres.

I believe that, following the Israeli-Palestinian agreement, we will move toward establishing diplomatic relations with other neighboring Arab countries such as Jordan, Syria, Lebanon, as well as the North African Magrheb countries and other Muslim countries. We hope that this will be a new era for the entire Middle East and a great opportunity for the democratic world.

****

Those who speak against the peace process must be able to provide answers to some very serious questions such as What are the alternatives? Should Israel become a nondemocratic binational state annexing two million Palestinians? Would we prefer dealing with Muslim Fundamentalists who will eventually gain a majority among Palestinians in the Territories? Should Israel renege on its agreement to reach a conciliation with the Palestinians as written and signed in the Camp David Accords?

Responsible leadership should deal with realpolitik. Its duty is to build a better future for its people through wisdom and courage. The people of the Middle East are entitled to better their lives and devote their resources and their human potential to achieve better health care, better economies, and better educations, rather than continue the wasteful process of hate and belligerency.

Now is the time for great leadership to take bold steps and make courageous decisions. Now is not the time for old rhetoric.

Excerpted from a speech delivered to the Friends of Tel-Aviv University, Chicago, Illinois, 8 September 1993.

Question of Palestine: United Nations 1993

One hundred years of conflict between Israelis and Palestinians have exacted a heavy price. The human loss has been tragic. The social and economic loss, enormous.

But now, we have witnessed a great victory of those with a vision for the future over those who are blinded by the past.

We believe that the Declaration of Principles signed on 13 September and the Letters of Mutual Recognition between Israel and the PLO are significant steps toward peace and prosperity in the Middle East.

This progress follows the peace treaty between Israel and Egypt, which shattered the stalemate in the Middle East, fourteen years ago.

Now, we have reached another historic crossroad. Change is inevitable. The old status quo could only bring more suffering and despair. The alternative to peace and reconciliation is war and devastation.

The time has come to depart from conflict and move toward cooperation, so Israelis and Palestinians can enjoy the fruits of peace and the shelter of security. In the words of Israeli Foreign Minister Shimon Peres, "Let us bid once and for all farewell to wars, to threats, to human misery. Let us bid farewell to enmity, and may there be no more victims on either side."

It is time to depart from violence and terror. It is time to establish good relations between Israel and its neighbors.

We are now working together, Israelis and Palestinians, according to the mutually agreed timetable, as we turn the agreement from principles into reality. This is not an easy task, but there is no other way but to walk the path that we have chosen. The interim period will provide needed time for the seeds of trust to grow.

Israeli Prime Minister Yitzhak Rabin said, "The basis for our advance and progress in the implementation of the agreement is that each side must keep its commitments." From these roots, mutual confidence will grow.

Far from the limelight, Israeli-Palestinian committees are hard at work, focusing on the details.

The Coordinating Committee is negotiating security arrangements and other modalities of the transfer of authority in Gaza and Jericho.

Of course, there are, and will be, ups and downs in the process; this is a time of transition. But now is the time to realize the simple truth: We can choose either painful compromise or perpetual conflict.

The implementation will succeed if both parties work persistently, pragmatically and professionally toward this end. I believe both sides are proceeding in this spirit, despite moments of hardship and outbreaks of violence.

A constructive atmosphere also marks our negotiations on economic matters. As we face the great challenges that lie ahead of us, progress toward economic development is essential.

Two weeks ago in Paris, the Economic Cooperation Committee began its work, guided by the principles of reciprocity, equity, and fair relationships.

The committee is exploring joint action in diverse fields: water, energy, industry and infrastructure, among others. Working groups have been established to specifically address these issues. Three subcommittees are meeting to deal with trade and labor, fiscal matters, and finance and banking. The work these groups do will become the economic foundations during the interim period.

We also seek progress in our negotiations with other partners. Israel desires a comprehensive peace, based on treaties with all our neighbors: Syria, Jordan, and Lebanon, as well as with the Gulf States and North African States, and with all other Arab and Moslem countries.

The United Nations should encourage peace by adopting an attitude that reflects the positive changes in the Middle East. Resolutions wielded as political weapons are relics of a bitter past. It is time for a change, it is time to move forward. Let us adopt resolutions that support the peace process and its accomplishments and indicate a wish for a better future.

As we continue the work of implementing the agreements, we confront many problems. Among the most severe are the continuous acts of terrorism designed to undermine the peace process and sow unrest and anarchy.

Some of these terrorists are driven by radical Islamic fanaticism.

Others are political opponents of the PLO, and some are rebellious members who have ignored their leadership's renunciation of terror.

In a prosperous environment, the fanatics would have no support because they rely on despair and recruit the despondent.

The international community should assist the Palestinians in the West Bank and Gaza through the transition period by helping improve social and economic conditions, by improving the infrastructure, expanding education and health centers, and by creating jobs that put more people to work.

In the short run, economic aid will finance services until other arrangements are made. In the long run, aid will spur growth and prosperity.

In October, the International Donors' Conference in Washington raised $2 billion in pledges for development in the territories. The United Nations established a high-level Task Force to achieve this same goal.

UN agencies are doing excellent work in the territories. UNDP has improved infrastructure and irrigation networks, and built a fishing port in Gaza. UNRWA has established clinics and hospitals and has done commendable work with children.

But the UN could do more. I repeat here the appeal made by Prime Minister Rabin to the Secretary-General of the United Nations: "Double the budget of the agencies which work in the territories. . . . double the effort."

We also appeal to the countries and organizations that promised economic aid: Meet your pledges. Time is precious.

The Palestinians have taken upon themselves an enormous responsibility. The challenges they face are immense. International assistance is critical, but it alone will not suffice. The Palestinians know that they themselves will have to create an economic environment that will generate growth and engender prosperity.

There is an answer to the "Question of Palestine." The answer is in the Declaration of Principles and in its implementation and should be left for the parties to resolve for themselves.

The United Nations and the member states have a historic responsibility to support this agreement. Help the Palestinians meet the enormous challenges, and encourage us all to stay on course: Mobilize resources; increase investment; avoid distraction; refrain from rhetoric; create a positive political and economic environment.

Help the peacemakers make their own peace.

Excerpted from a speech delivered in the United Nations General Assembly, 30 November 1993.

The Massacre in Hebron: First Security Council Speech

Israel regrets and condemns the criminal murder of Palestinian worshippers in Hebron. We express our sincerest condolences to the families of those killed, and we wish all those wounded a speedy and complete recovery.

In an appeal to Israelis and Palestinians alike, the President of the State of Israel, Ezer Weizman, said, "At this difficult time, I call upon all the people of this land, leaders, clergy, Jews and Arabs, Christians and Moslems to grieve together over every needless loss of life."

Our Prime Minister Yitzhak Rabin spoke by telephone with PLO Chairman Yasser Arafat. Prime Minister Rabin conveyed the sorrow of the Israeli government and people to Chairman Arafat and to the Palestinian people. He said, "As an Israeli, I am ashamed of this deranged, brutal act." I join the Prime Minister in this sentiment, as do the overwhelming majority of Israelis.

The fanatic individual—I repeat, individual—who committed the violence sought not only to kill people, but also to kill the chances for peace between Israelis and Palestinians. Extremists on both sides believe that they can derail the peace process by creating a vicious cycle of violence and bloodshed.

They are wrong. We believe that all sides know that we have crossed the point of no return on our way to a new era of peace, security, and cooperation. Difficulties will arise. Obstacles will have to be overcome. We were all reminded of this sad truth by the latest events. But the only way to put an end to the violence is through peace and reconciliation. There simply is no alternative. We all have a responsibility to the future not to walk away from the historic opportunity that stands before us.

For this reason it is imperative that all people, Arabs and Jews alike, act with the utmost restraint, despite the sorrow, the grief, and the anger.

Israelis, of all people, understand the pain of losing innocent lives. It is with this understanding that we call for restraint. We, the Israeli people, have faced decades of violence by fanatic Palestinians and others. We have mourned hundreds of Israelis killed in terrorist attacks.

I will not repeat here the long list of such incidents. Let me just say that since the signing of the Declaration of Principles on 13 September 1993, 33 Israelis have been killed in terrorist attacks in Israel and the territories and 213 have been wounded. These acts were committed not only by individuals, but also by organized terrorist groups. Despite this, we have not lost hope for peace; we never came to the conclusion that there were justifications to abandon the search for reconciliation between our peoples.

Some Palestinian and Arab leaders have said that they want Israel to change its policies. Allow me to bring to your attention some relevant facts on this matter.

Following the formation of the present government on 13 July 1992, Israel made far-reaching changes in its order of national priorities:

- The government of Israel stopped construction of new settlements in the territories.
- We reallocated resources away from the territories and into Israel.
- The government of Israel decided to recognize the PLO as the representative of the Palestinian people and commence negotiations with the PLO within the Middle East peace process.
- Israel signed the Declaration of Principles on Interim Self-Government Arrangements with the PLO on 13 September 1993.
- We announced our readiness to negotiate without preconditions a permanent settlement with the Palestinians by no later than the third year of the interim period.
- And we announced our readiness to negotiate a peace treaty with Syria on the basis of territorial compromise.

At two meetings held on 25 and 27 February, the cabinet discussed the massacre in Hebron and authorized a number of steps.

First, a Commission of Inquiry headed by the chief justice of the Supreme Court has been established to fully investigate the massacre.

Second, a series of measures has been taken against radical elements among the Israeli residents of the territories. These measures include:

- the imposition of administrative detentions;
- the extension of restraining orders and supervisory orders

against the entry of certain persons into the territories and especially into the Hebron area;
- and the disarming of specific individuals and the cancellation of their permits to carry weapons.

Third, the attorney general will explore and propose options for outlawing the radical organizations "Kach" and "Kahane Chai."

Fourth, the government decided to release up to one thousand Palestinian detainees and prisoners within the coming week.

Fifth, new security and prayer arrangements will be made for the Tomb of the Patriarchs in Hebron. The site will be reopened when these new arrangements are made.

Sixth, the government will provide compensation to the families of the victims.

Unfortunately, some Palestinian leaders have called the government's decisions "empty, hollow, and superficial." This is very regrettable.

I want to stress here that the government of Israel is fully committed to doing its utmost to protect Arabs and Jews alike. Measures are being taken to halt the activities of all radical elements that are a source of incitement in the territories.

The Israel Defense Forces will continue to do all they can to maintain public order and to prevent further incidents and bloodshed. Once the implementation of the Israeli-Palestinian agreement begins, the Palestinian police will take its part in ensuring security.

We believe that the only sincere solution to the conflict between Israelis and Palestinians is to enhance the implementation of the agreement between Israel and the PLO. We all have to focus on accelerating the progress toward peace.

Foreign Minister Shimon Peres said that, "peace is the true answer to the hate mongers and the sowers of grief."

Faithful and speedy implementation of the agreement on Interim Self-Government Arrangements will frustrate the plans of extremists and swell the ranks of those who believe that Israelis and Palestinians can and should live in peace, dignity, and mutual respect.

The Security Council has a responsibility to support these proponents of peace by calling for accelerated progress toward implementing the Israeli-Palestinian agreement.

I will conclude with these words, delivered by Prime Minister Rabin to Israel's Knesset:

> I say to the Palestinians . . . we understand your feelings, and suffer this terrible tragedy together with you. We identify with the heavy

sorrow, the distress, and the tears, and we know that even when peace will come, both you and we will bear the scars of war.

We call upon you to return to the negotiating table, to resume the talks. We shall sit down and continue the negotiations. For after the blood, after the tears, that which we have so long sought and dreamed about may lie waiting in the near future: To put an end to one hundred years of war and terrorism, and to begin to exist, to begin to live, like all nations.

Excerpted from a speech delivered in the United Nations Security Council, 28 February 1994.

We Will Not Despair

This is a significant and decisive time for all of us—Jews, Arabs; Israelis, Palestinians. Last Friday, 25 February, at 5:30 in the morning, a deranged individual entered the Tomb of the Patriarchs to shoot like a madman at hundreds of innocent people who were deep in prayer. Acting alone, he killed tens and wounded hundreds. He himself was killed on the spot by the people there.

This insane murder shocked all of us.

Allow me to say in all modesty and sorrow: The man who committed this massacre removed himself from the Community of Israel. So have all those who have supported his actions.

In the words of Israel's Chief Sephardi Rabbi Eliahu Bakshi Doron: "I am stunned, shocked. To say that I condemn the act is an understatement. I am simply ashamed that a Jew carried out such a villainous act, and I am distressed that it is viewed as the act of a religious person."

And in the words of Chief Ashkenazi Rabbi Yisrael Meir Lau: "The entire Jewish people always opposed murder and bloodshed. No other nation has suffered as much from murder, hatred and enmity as we have. Therefore, it is especially painful to us that a Jew should have committed this indiscriminate murder of worshippers. The attacker did not act in the name of the Jewish faith."

Israelis, of all people, understand the pain of losing innocent lives. We, the Israeli people, have faced decades of violence by fanatic Palestinians and others. We have mourned hundreds of Israelis killed in terrorist attacks.

Despite this, we never lost hope for peace; we never came to the conclusion that they were justifications to abandon the search for reconciliation between our peoples.

Even when hundreds of Palestinians were killed by Islamic fundamentalists, we condemned the murders and expressed our sorrow.

I do not remember hearing the Palestinians making these types of statements, either before the signing of the Declaration of Principles or after it. But this never made us respond with silence when terror struck them. It never made us deny our profound respect for life. As Jews and Israelis, we grieve over every loss of human life. We will remain true to our faith and our heritage. If both sides could respond to violence with condemnation and expressions of regret, then the peace process would be greatly enhanced.

If we despair of making peace and allow the situation to deteriorate, we will have handed a victory to fanatics on both sides. We will have handed a victory to radicals from Kach and radicals from Hamas. It will be a victory of those who are trapped in the past over those who look to the future.

We will not despair in the face of calamities. We will continue on the road to peace and to a better future, guided by the Jewish ethics and human values that our heritage has bestowed upon us.

Excerpted from a speech delivered to the New York Board of Rabbis on 3 March 1994.

The Massacre in Hebron: Second Security Council Speech

Israel believes that all sides should dedicate themselves from now on to resuming and accelerating the peace process. This is the only way to change the reality and create a new future for Israelis, Palestinians, and neighboring Arab states.

Therefore, we share the Security Council's support for the peace process currently under way and call for the implementation of the Declaration of Principles, signed by Israel and the PLO, without delay.

My government welcomes the steps announced today to get the peace process back on track soon.

The letters of invitation to the Madrid Peace Conference, sent by the cosponsors to the participants on 18 October 1991, constitute the terms of reference upon which the peace process is based. Within this framework, Israel and the PLO signed the Declaration of Principles on 13 September 1993, as well as the Cairo Agreement on 9 February 1994. We believe that we have to act within the framework of the agreed peace process and those agreements.

Security must be guaranteed for all residents of the territories, Jews and Arabs alike. We can best achieve this by implementing the Declaration of Principles. Article Eight of the Declaration stipulates, and I quote: "In order to guarantee public order and internal security for the Palestinians of the West Bank and the Gaza Strip, the Council will establish a strong police force, while Israel will continue to carry the responsibility for defending against external threats, as well as the responsibility for overall security of Israelis for the purpose of safeguarding their internal security and public order."

The Declaration of Principles provides for the possibility of a temporary international or foreign presence, "as agreed upon." We maintain that nothing in the present resolution prejudices this provision in the Declaration of Principles.

Following the tragic event that took place in Hebron on 25 February, Israel strongly condemned the massacre and took several unprecedented measures.

At its weekly meeting Sunday, 13 March 1994, the government of Israel declared that the Kach and the Kahane Chai movements are terrorist organizations.

This announcement applies to these organizations as well as to any group of people acting to achieve aims of that nature, which the above-mentioned groups have been working to achieve.

The government of Israel also reaffirmed that at present, as in the past, it is solely responsible, by means of the Israel Defense Forces and the Israel Police, for the security of all inhabitants, both Jewish and Arab, of the territories. The government of Israel intends to take all measures necessary to ensure security, within the boundaries of the law.

The government of Israel stated that with the completion of the negotiations on the Gaza-Jericho Agreement, a Palestinian police force will be established that will take responsibility for the security of the Arab residents of those areas. During the transition period, the necessary measures will be taken to ensure that a security vacuum is not created.

****

The reference to Jerusalem in this resolution is not compatible with the Declaration of Principles, whereby both parties have agreed to address the issue not later than the beginning of the third year of the interim period. The reference to Jerusalem in the resolution is also at variance with Israel's position regarding the city's present and future status: Jerusalem will remain united under Israeli sovereignty as our eternal capital.

Israel has suffered from terrorism throughout all the years of its existence. Yet we never abandoned our quest for peace. Now, as well, Israel remains fully committed to advance towards peace on the basis of Security Council Resolutions 242 and 338, and the Declaration of Principles signed by Israel and the PLO.

Time is precious. We should not miss this historic opportunity. We call upon the Palestinians and all other participants in the negotiations, Syria, Jordan, and Lebanon, to return to the peace talks in order to carry on with the essential task of establishing peace and security in our region.

Excerpted from the speech delivered in the United Nations Security Council, 18 March 1994.

Trapped in the Past

Since the signing of the Declaration of Principles in Washington, the media have tended to portray the debate in Israel as a disagreement over matters of security, and security alone.

But the disagreement between the government and opposition is not solely a dispute over terrorism and security arrangements.

Rather, we are engaged in a debate over fundamental issues of national direction: Is a secure peace based on territorial compromise preferable to a continuation of the Arab-Israeli conflict?

Should Israel continue to rule over two million Palestinians against their will at the risk becoming a binational or nondemocratic state through annexation of the territories, or should it attempt to arrive at a situation where they are responsible for running their own lives?

The debate both in Israel and neighboring Arab countries is between those with a vision for the future and those trapped in the mindset of the past. That mindset is concerned more with military responses to symptoms of the conflict rather than social, economic, and political attempts to eliminate its root causes.

The breakthrough achieved with the Palestinians is already being followed by a gradual improvement in our relations with Arab and Moslem states. I believe this will eventually lead to normalization and peace with our neighbors. New opportunities for regional cooperation will then widen the economic horizons of the entire region.

This, of course, is predicated on the removal of the Arab boycott. The boycott is not only an obstacle to peace, but also the major obstacle to free trade in the Middle East. The boycott is holding back the entire region.

We still face obstacles such as Islamic fundamentalism, radicalism, and the proliferation of weapons of mass destruction. But the advances in the peace process may signify a growing political maturity in the Middle East, where economic and rational self-interest supersede ideology and emotion as the basis of decisions.

We have a rare opportunity to transform the region and to make real progress toward peace and prosperity. As we move forward on this track, it is important not to lose perspective. The dispute between the two schools of thought in Israel is not about security measures—it is not about early warning stations, positioning of troops, or other technical issues. We all are concerned about those. Rather, it is a substantial debate over the country's course for the future.

Excerpted from an article originally published in *The Jerusalem Post International Edition*, 5 March 1994.

Israelis Debate Not Risks, but the Future

I read with great interest "The New Palestine" A. M. Rosenthal's 8 March column, warning of Palestinian espectations of statehood since the Declaration of Principles was signed in Washington on 13 Sept. He seems to view a Palestinian entity as a great risk for Israel.

I believe that he and others who share his views have a responsibility to answer some basic questions: What is the alternative to the present policy? Do you prefer that Israel rule over two million Palestinians against their will, without political rights forever?

Do you doubt Israel's military strength so much, even after repeated victories against Arab coalitions, that you view a demilitarized Palestinian entity that has signed a peace treaty with Israel as a serious threat to Israeli security?

It goes without saying that any peace agreement will include, to use Mr. Rosenthal's words, "specific important guarantees" for Israel's security. But the attention Mr. Rosenthal focuses on these issues diverts him from addressing fundamental questions like those asked above.

Letter to the editor of the *New York Times,* published 13 March 1994.

Question of Palestine: United Nations 1994

These are fateful days for Israel, for the Palestinians, and for the entire Middle East. On the one hand, we are gradually bringing about a great change: from conflict to understanding, from bitter division to advancement. On the other hand, violent extremists are trying to destroy the progress we have made already. By killing innocent human beings they are trying to kill the chance for peace and normalization.

I shall refrain from responding to the unfortunate statement made here by the speaker for the PLO. Some of his statements were totally unfounded. I would like to make just one comment, to set the record straight.

Today, forty-seven years ago, the United Nations General Assembly decided on the establishment of two states in British Mandatory Palestine: the State of Israel and an Arab state. The Jews living under the British Mandate accepted this resolution and established the State of Israel on 14 May 1948. The Palestinians, unfortunately, with the support of all the Arab countries, rejected the resolution and launched a war on the State of Israel.

At the war's end a year later the State of Israel survived. Some Palestinians became citizens of Israel, some became citizens of Jordan, which captured the West Bank, some became subjects of Egypt, which captured the Gaza Strip, and some became refugees in Arab countries.

I hope that we have learned the lessons of the past and now turn to build a new future. Although I have some doubts about this notion after hearing the speaker for the PLO.

For all peoples of the Middle East, especially for the Palestinians and their leadership, these are decisive days.

The events of the past fourteen months represent an unprecedented turning point. Even if this is just the beginning, even if many obstacles must still be overcome—the old status quo has been shattered forever.

On 13 September 1993, Israel and the PLO signed the Declaration of Principles. This agreement marks a watershed in the history of relations between Israelis and Palestinians. The DOP rests upon several basic tenets: mutual recognition, direct negotiation without preconditions as the only framework to advance peace, and an interim period for confidence-building and for an orderly transition to the permanent status.

The signing of the Declaration of Principles set in motion a process that we hope will gradually lead to a resolution of the issues dividing us. . . . It has been an impressive journey toward fulfilling a common goal: enabling the Palestinians to assume responsibility for their own lives. Much has been accomplished in a relatively short time.

Nonetheless, groups such as Hamas and the Islamic Jihad continue to embrace violence. They are aiming to derail the progress toward peace, stability, and development. As they pursue their terrorist activities, these groups receive support and encouragement from Iran and other countries. In recent months, suicide bombers and fanatic gunmen have targeted innocent Israeli civilians and have wrought indiscriminate havoc and bloodshed. Lately, fundamentalist radicals affiliated with these groups have rioted against the Palestinian Authority and the Palestinian Police in the Gaza Strip.

Combating terrorism and violence is essential for increasing security. This, in turn, is essential for increasing trust and cooperation.

The struggle is between those who are trapped in the past and those who are trying to build a better future.

For the builders of peace, the immediate tasks are clear.

- We must enable the Palestinian Authority to meet its responsibilities under the Declaration of Principles.
- All parties to the peace process must cooperate in the fight against terrorism. We cannot allow those who would drag us back to the past to succeed in their vision of renewed war and bloodshed. We have to curb the forces that are supporting the fanatic, radical groups.
- Assistance from the donor countries is crucial for developing infrastructure, education, health, sanitation, and employment in the Gaza Strip, the Jericho area, and eventually in other areas in the West Bank. The Palestinian Authority and the donor countries need to find ways to ensure that funds are quickly transferred to such projects. The donor countries have now convened in Brussels to discuss this issue. We hope that all commitments will soon be fulfilled.
- The entire international community must join in the effort to improve the basic conditions in Gaza, Jericho, and eventually in other areas of the West Bank. Every man, woman and child

in these places must be able to enjoy the fruits of peace. If peace is to be rooted firmly in the hearts and minds of the people, it must touch every person individually. Its blessings need to be felt in every house, every school, every workplace, and every community. In this way, more and more people will understand that peace is the best security. It is the key to assuming responsibility for oneself and for one's future; and it is the true road to economic, social, and human advancement.

I would appeal to the Palestinian representatives to leave the issues that relate to the permanent settlement to their appropriate time, as was agreed by the parties. None of these are relevant to the present stage of negotiations. Let us concentrate on building understanding and cementing the agreement between us.

Israel, for its part, remains committed to the peace process with the Palestinians. Only if both parties meet their obligations under the agreements signed, can we create the better future that is our common goal.

Excerpted from a speech delivered in the United Nations General Assembly, 29 November 1994.

Facing Reality

Today, Israelis and concerned people all over the world are questioning many fundamental issues. To those who ask, "How can you trust Arafat," I answer: Do you have a better alternative?

We have to face reality. For the long run, we have four policy choices: transfer, annexation, the status quo or peaceful coexistence.

Our first option, *transfer,* would be to expel the people from the territories. This would be inhuman, and to be inhuman would contradict the moral foundations of Israeli society.

Turning to our second alternative, we have *annexation*. But what would this lead to? Annexation would replace Israel with a binational state. In other words, Israel as we know it would cease to exist. Therefore, the policy of annexation is essentially short sighted.

Now, what would happen if we maintained the status quo forever? This would create an apartheid-like situation where the Palestinians would never be granted equal rights. How much better, how much more productive, to harness Israel's great energies and resources for development rather than for controlling two million people against their wills. The answer is self-evident.

So, my friends, what are we left with? The only rational option that was ever really ours to pursue is *peaceful coexistence*—but a coexistence based on Israel's security needs.

Since the Biltmore Conference in 1942, the Jewish leaders have adopted the partition approach. The pre-state Jewish community, known as the Yishuv, and its leader David Ben-Gurion, accepted the UN resolution adopted on 29 November 1947. They agreed to establish Israel in part of Mandatory Palestine, not because of territory, but because of people. But the Arabs rejected the proposal and tried to abolish it by force. Israel survived.

In 1967, we faced another existential threat, but Israel won the Six Day War and became the so-called "occupier" of Sinai, the Golan, the Gaza Strip, and the West Bank. It is significant that the West Bank and Gaza were never independent, but were controlled by Jordan and Egypt before 1967. Just as Jerusalem was never the capital of any other state—only of Israel, in ancient times and today.

The course we have chosen is not new. Rather, it has guided the Jewish leadership since the 1930s. Unfortunately, the Arabs rejected it then. But now, following the end of the Cold War, and faced with Israel's strength, determination, and sustained initiatives for peace, they are ready for peace and cooperation.

Excerpted from an address delivered to the Harvard Club in New York, 31 January 1995.

Calling Iran to Account

These are sad, tragic days for all of us.

Nineteen young people have been lost to their families and to us all. Scores of wounded lie suffering in hospitals throughout Israel. And while our injured cry and our dead scream out, shouts of joy are heard in the streets of Gaza. Thousands of radical extremists gathered at the homes of the terrorists to celebrate.

Since the signing of the Declaration of Principles, 110 Israelis have been killed in terrorist attacks. The fundamentalist groups Hamas and Islamic Jihad are responsible for almost all of them.

The leader of the Damascus-based faction of Islamic Jihad that carried out Sunday's attack, Fathi Shekaki, has boasted of his close ties with Iran. He claims that Iranian support for his organization and Hamas amounts to about twenty million dollars. Recently, he announced that a group of seventy terrorists are being trained to commit suicide attacks against Israel.

We insist that the Palestinian Authority uphold its commitments to curb violence, to imprison murderers, to disarm the militants. They have been given the means. They are obligated to do it.

On the other hand, the response of the international community has been encouraging. Both the Security Council and the Secretary-General of the United Nations condemned the attack. The Secretary-General delivered a statement yesterday in which he "condemns in the strongest possible terms this abhorrent act of terrorism." Both extended their condolences to the families of those killed and wished a speedy recovery to the wounded. This was the first time in the history of the United Nations that the Security Council as a whole adopted a statement condemning terrorism committed against Israelis.

These reactions followed a letter I sent to the Secretary-General, which has been circulated as an official UN document. In the letter, I described the Iranian connection to the fundamentalist terrorism. Who is supporting Islamic Jihad and Hamas? Who supplies them with financial means? Who provides them with weapons? With training? With spiritual guidance and inspiration?

Iran must be held accountable for its actions. The blood of countless victims of terrorism is on its hands. Through its proxies, it threatens almost every moderate state in the Middle East. We have to insist that the international community cut off all ties and all assistance to Iran. Let them give no sanction to terrorism and no quarter to its sponsors. When I read that a former superpower is helping build a nuclear reactor there, I am outraged. When I read that other Western countries continue their economic and commercial ties with Iran, I am outraged. There can be no excuse for such a shortsighted policy.

We must praise the president of the United States for the courageous steps he took to curb the terrorist organizations here in America. We call upon all enlightened countries to follow the American government's action. Terrorism is an international threat, and the entire international community must fight it.

The Islamic fundamentalists are trying to prevent us from achieving a better future—a future of coexistence, peace, and security. But they will not succeed.

At such an emotional time, it is not hard to lose of sight your own long-term interests. Anger and despair can easily get the better of you. But there is no alternative but to pursue peace. Just as there is no alternative but to guarantee security; and to demand that the Palestinians uphold their end of the agreement. It must be respected by both sides.

These are difficult days—sad and tragic. We have known such days before. But there is hope.

This is a meeting of unity—of solidarity with the families and friends of the victims and with the Israeli people.

It is a gathering of *Kol Yisrael Arevim Zeh L'zeh*. It is a gathering of *Am Yisrael Chai.*

Address delivered on 25 January 1995, at a memorial service for victims of the terrorist attack Beit Lid, near Netanya.

The "Islamic Bomb"

Despite the progress toward peace—maybe even as a result—dark forces, trapped in the past, are committed to destroying any possibility for a better future for everyone in the region. We saw this last week, in the barbaric attack that took the lives of twenty young Israelis at the bus stop in Beit Lid, near Netanya.

That act of terrorism is part of a campaign by radical Islamic fundamentalists to take control of the entire region. Their aim is to destabilize moderate Arab countries like Jordan, Egypt, and Tunisia; they have already seized power in Sudan and are on the verge of success in Algeria. Just yesterday a car bomb killed thirty-eight and injured 256 in there. Their aim is to wipe Israel off the map, and their jihad spreads terror and death all over the world.

The terrorist organizations like Hamas, Islamic Jihad, and the Hizballah do not function alone. Without Iran and other countries they would be powerless. The Shekaki faction of Islamic Jihad claimed responsibility for the attack last week from his office *in Damascus.* And Iran backs him and the others with support, guidance, training, weapons, financing, and inspiration.

Iran poses the most significant long-term danger to the stability of the Middle East. As you all know, Iran is on the verge of developing nuclear weapons. Even without outside help, our intelligence projects——and this is confirmed by U.S. reports as well—that in only seven to fifteen years, Iran will hold a nuclear bomb in its grip. And this is without outside assistance.

But the fact is Russia is being paid $800 million to complete an Iranian nuclear power plant. Expertise and material are pouring in from China and North Korea. Western countries continue to maintain economic ties and provide dual-use technologies. And if this trend continues, we can expect that Iran will achieve nuclear capability even sooner. The danger is clear and present.

Following the terrorist attack in Israel last week, I sent a letter to the Secretary-General and the Security Council and called on all countries to cut ties and assistance to Iran. We cannot afford to be shortsighted. There is a direct connection between Iran's opposition to the peace process, sponsorship of terrorism, and nuclear ambitions.

The international community bears a solemn responsibility to ensure that Iran will not be able to cast a nuclear shadow over the Middle East. If Iran builds a nuclear arsenal, no one—no one—is safe. It doesn't matter if you are sitting in Tel Aviv, Riyadh or New York.

Let's not fool ourselves and think that any treaties will stop Iran from pursuing its nuclear program. The Non-Proliferation Treaty has not stopped Iran. It didn't stop Iraq either. Israel in 1981 and the United States in 1991 stopped Iraq. But even though NPT was not worth the ink Iraq and Iran used to sign it, some countries are increasing pressure on Israel to sign the treaty. Yesterday, the Preparatory Committee for the Extension of NPT terminated its session in New York without coming to an agreement. In April, the full conference will meet at the UN. As the date approaches, we can expect the issue to heat up. People in the media are asking me: "Why won't Israel sign the NPT?"

Israel always has and will continue to support the establishment of a nuclear-weapon-free zone in the region. However, as long as Israel is directly threatened by Iran, Iraq, Libya, and others, we cannot endanger our very existence. Why have we never confirmed or denied whether we have nuclear weapons? Because we have found that, in our neighborhood, experience has taught us very well—this is best form of deterrence available. Therefore, a nuclear-weapon-free zone could only be established after comprehensive peace is achieved. We will pursue it. We are committed to it. I believe we will reach it.

Excerpted from an address delivered to the Harvard Club in New York, 31 January 1995.

On the Meaning of Jerusalem

No one is more sensitive to the meaning of Jerusalem than the Jewish people. Ever since King David established it as our capital

3,000 years ago, Jerusalem has been the essence of our nationhood. Jerusalem was never the capital of any other people. The Caliphs ruled it for centuries. But they never made it their capital. Neither did the Mamelukes or the Ottomans.

When the sites of many of today's great capitals were only fields of passage for nomads, Jerusalem was our capital. Even then, it was the object of pilgrimage for our people—three times a year. Our kings ruled from her palaces. Our priests served God in her Temple. Our prophets preached justice in her streets. Even then, before many of the nations on this earth were born, Jerusalem was the national, political, cultural, religious and spiritual center of the Jewish people.

The continuous Jewish presence in the city began 3,000 years ago and lasted, unbroken, to this very day. Even under foreign domination and persecution, we maintained a significant and vital presence in Jerusalem. Indeed, since the second half of the nineteenth century, Jews have constituted the majority of the city's inhabitants.

For Jews living in exile for 2,000 years, the centrality of Jerusalem sustained us as a people and gave us the hope to carry on through the darkest days. The words "Next year in Jerusalem" were always on the lips and in the hearts of Jews. The words of the psalmist best explain this devotion. "If I forget thee, O Jerusalem, let my right hand forget her cunning. If I do not remember thee, let my tongue cleave to the roof of my mouth." This is the prayer of every child born to the Jewish people—in every age, in every place: in New York, Moscow, Buenos Aires, London, Paris, Rome, Prague, Rabat, Cairo . . . and Jerusalem.

We are sensitive to the importance of Jerusalem to Christians and Moslems. And we are proud that since 1967, Jerusalem is open to pilgrims and worshippers of all religions, and each faith freely administers its own holy sites.

The centrality of Jerusalem in the soul of the Jewish people has been expressed in many ways. Our psalmists praised it in songs of ascent, and mourned its destruction in songs of lamentation. One hundred years ago, the Jewish people found inspiration in a new song, but with an ancient theme.

> As long as, deep in the heart,
> The soul of a Jew yearns,
> And towards the East,
> An eye looks to Zion,
> Then our hope is not yet lost.

The hope of two thousand years:
To be a free people in our land,
The land of Zion and Jerusalem."

This old-new song is the national anthem of the State of Israel, "Hatikva," "The Hope."

In the words of Prime Minister Yitzhak Rabin, "The policy of all the governments of Israel was and is Jerusalem is united under Israel's sovereignty, the capital of Israel and the heart of the Jewish people forever." And further, "We have always promised and ensured freedom of worship for all religions and free access to all holy places."

There is no contradiction between this policy and bilateral agreements Israel has signed, including the Declaration of Principles with the PLO, and we are committed to this agreement.

In the DOP, Israel and the PLO agreed that issues relating to the permanent status will be negotiated by the parties themselves in a later stage. Moreover, there is no contradiction between the peace process and continued development in Jerusalem for the benefit of all its residents—both Jewish and Arab. We do not accept the proposition that the natural and continued development of Jerusalem—or any other city—can or should be arrested. Certainly, if one looks at the Declaration of Principles, one will find no reference to any prohibition of development activity in Jerusalem.

If the leadership of the PLO feels otherwise, then the matter should be appropriately addressed in the framework of our bilateral negotiations. Indeed, Israel and the PLO agreed that differences and disputes arising out of the application or interpretation of the agreements, should be settled between the parties themselves according to the process detailed in both the DOP and the Gaza-Jericho Agreement.

Accordingly, we believe that any attempt to address this issue outside the agreed-upon framework stands in contradiction to the letter and spirit of the agreements signed by Israel and the PLO and to the principles of the peace process.

Continued progress toward peace should be the main concern of all parties. We all must travel the road to peace with determination. Let all give it the highest priority. Especially because the road is so difficult and the obstacles are so many.

The Middle East has come a long way in the past years. The agreements between Israel and the PLO; the implementation of the first stage, despite the continuous terrorism waged by the enemies of peace; the Israel-Jordan peace treaty; the establishment of working relations between Israel and other countries of the Middle East and North Africa; the basis for regional economic cooperation that has been laid by the Casablanca Conference and the multilateral negotiations.

Now, we have to continue building on this foundation, to do our utmost so that a comprehensive peace be achieved. This is our conviction, our commitment, our hope.

Excerpted from a speech delivered in the United Nations Security Council, 12 May 1995.

4

Shaping the Future

The Situation in the Middle East: United Nations 1992

THE Middle East is undergoing changes that might lead either to peace and progress or to continuing unrest. Yet it remains a region brimming with conflicts, one of which is between Israel and a number of neighboring Arab states and the Palestinians. But this is neither the primary nor the only conflict in the region.

There are other sources of tension in the region, such as the actions of terrorist groups; the rise of radical fundamentalism; the clashes in Iraq between the government and the Kurdish and Shiite minorities; the massive Syrian presence in Lebanon; and the enormous arsenals of weapons in Iran and Iraq. All of these are a threat to the peace of the region and to the prospects for further human and economic development.

The time has come for us, who live in the region, to address not just the symptoms but the disease. The true way to go about this is to encourage the bilateral and multilateral peace negotiations and to strengthen support for democratization.

We welcome the participation of Syria, Jordan, and Lebanon, for the first time, in direct negotiations with Israel toward peace treaties. This has been our aspiration since the establishment of the State of Israel. For since our rebirth as a state, we have been subjected to war and aggression. On 15 May 1948, when the British Mandate in Palestine came to an end, seven Arab armies invaded Israel. At the time, I was twelve years old. I remember well the fear we had when the invading Iraqi Army was as close as four miles from the village where I had grown up. In his memoirs, *In the Cause of Peace,* H. E. Mr. Trygve Lie, the first secretary-general of the United Nations, described the Arab assault after the founding of the State of Israel as follows: "During the next hours and days, events crowded upon us. The Arab states launched their invasion of Palestine with the end of the Mandate. This was clear aggression. . . . "

Despite the attacks upon us, we held firm to our hope for peace. This hope was embodied in our Declaration of Independence, which states,

> We extend our hand to all neighboring states and their peoples in an offer of peace and good neighborliness, and appeal to them to establish bonds of cooperation and mutual help with the sovereign Jewish people settled in its own land. The State of Israel is prepared to do its share in a common effort for the advancement of the entire Middle East.

The road toward building a new future for the Middle East passes through peace treaties. We must build a new kind of relationship among the people and states of the region. This will be the main test of statesmanship for the leaders of the countries in our region. In addition, it holds the promise of a breakthrough away from the apocalyptic dangers of a new confrontation and toward a better life for everyone.

Next week, the bilateral negotiations will resume in Washington between the delegations of Israel and Syria, Jordan, Lebanon, and the Palestinians. The two cosponsors of the peace process, the United States and the Russian Federation, have our appreciation and gratitude for their continuing efforts to encourage and promote peace. All of us know that the issues in the talks are complex and that the negotiations are taking place after many year of hostility and alienation. However, if all the parties adhere to the conviction that peace is vital, I believe that agreements will be reached and that peace will come.

As was stated by the Prime Minister of Israel, Mr. Yitzhak Rabin, it would greatly help the peace process if President Assad of Syria and our Prime Minister would meet in Damascus or in Jerusalem to discuss ways to achieve progress toward peace and security. The same appeal has been made to King Hussein of Jordan. On this occasion, I would like to wish him good health and a quick recovery.

While the bilateral negotiations aim to achieve peace treaties and reconciliation among the parties concerned, the multilateral negotiations are an essential step toward building the new Middle East. As outlined in the invitation to the Madrid peace conference, the purpose of the multilateral talks is to address issues that are of common concern to all people in the region: arms control, refugees, the environment, water resources, and regional economic cooperation. These are issues whose importance transcends boundaries and conflicts. They must be dealt with if we are to meet the challenges that lie ahead. Israel welcomes the progress made thus far in the multilateral talks, in which the United Nations is a full participant, and we hope that the talks will continue to move in a positive direction.

I would like to propose the creation of a forum of the United Nations ambassadors from the countries of the Middle East. The forum would provide us with a means for working together, in coordination with the specialized agencies of the United Nations, to promote good will through innovative programs. For example, we could formulate educational projects for our children and youth to promote better understanding of cultural differences, and to encourage tolerance and coexistence. The agreed upon projects could then be developed and implemented by UNICEF and other agencies, with the cooperation of the countries involved. This might be a useful contribution toward creating an atmosphere of tolerance and mutual respect among all the peoples of the region.

Peace and democracy—these are the two ingredients that the Middle East needs most desperately. With them, our region can flower and prosper. Without them, we face a bleak and gloomy future.

I feel obliged to share with you our deep concern following the extensive racist and anti-Semitic outbursts in many places. It is our moral obligation to raise our voice and to call upon every enlightened individual, society, and government, to condemn and fight these immoral phenomena. It is our duty and our mission to condemn this threat without hesitation and to put an end to it.

On this occasion, I would also like to stress that the plight of oppressed Jewish communities in some of the countries in our region is close to our hearts. We shall spare no effort to ensure their right to reunite with the Jewish people. We shall not rest until they are free. Our thoughts and prayers are with them at all times.

As of now, six Israeli soldiers remain missing in action: Ron Arad, Yehuda Katz, Zachary Baumel, Zvi Feldman, Joseph Fink, and Rachamim Alsheikh. We would like to thank the Secretary-General of the United Nations for his efforts to return them home. We call upon those countries and organizations holding them to abide by international law and to display humanitarian sensitivity in order to prevent further suffering by the soldiers and their families and friends. Let our sons come home.

Many of us from all sides of the borders and from all peoples—Israelis, Arabs, Jews, Druze, and others—have lost friends and relatives in the long and painful path of conflict. The time has come for all of us to learn the lesson. The time has come to build a better future for us and for coming generations. The time has come for peace.

Excerpted from a speech delivered in the United Nations General Assembly, 4 December 1992.

Economic Progress

There has been great progress in the economic, technological, and scientific relationship between Israel and the United States. This very positive development is exemplified by the figures on the trade balance between Israel and the United States. Israeli exports to the United States exceeded Israeli imports from the United States in 1992. Our exports to the United States in 1992 were 3.8 billion dollars. United States exports to Israel in 1992 amounted to 3.4 billion dollars.

As Irwin Meltzer told us, Israeli companies trading on the stock exchange here in the United States, mobilized over one billion dollars in 1992 for investments, mainly in Israel. This is a very *promising* development. *But the potential is still much greater.*

We hope to become a full partner with the Free Trade Area to be formed among the United States, Mexico, and Canada—we hope to enter a new phase once a breakthrough is achieved and peace will reign among Israel, the neighboring Arab countries, and the Palestinians.

We have a competitive ability that will be fully expressed when the geopolitical situation will change.

It reminds me of the story about two people who were walking in the jungle one day. They saw a tiger from a distance, and one of them started to take off his shoes and put on a pair of sneakers. So his friend turned to him and said, "do you really believe that you will run faster than the tiger?" To which he replied, "I don't think I will run faster than the tiger. But all I have to do is run faster than you, and that *will* be enough. . . . "

Israel does not seek to run faster than the United States or Japan or Germany. It will be enough if we can run faster than some other countries and *fully exercise our comparative advantages* in various sectors.

Now is perhaps a onetime historical opportunity to achieve peace. We must not miss it!

Excerpted from a speech delivered to the America-Israel Chamber of Commerce and Industry on 18 May 1993.

The Potentials of Peace

This conference exemplifies the substantial and dramatic changes sweeping the world now. It stresses the need to prepare ourselves for the twenty-first century. It gives a clear message in support of regional and international cooperation. It advocates the openness and free exchange of views, ideas, and trade.

And it goes along with the encouraging, new developments in the Middle East.

On 13 September, on the South Lawn of the White House, a new era in the Middle East began to take shape. An agreed Declaration of Principles was signed by Israel and the PLO. This new era may ensure the people of our region and the world a better future, a season of peace.

The following day, Israel and Jordan signed an agreed joint agenda for peace. We are witnessing a watershed in the history of the Middle East. It is a crossroads in the one hundred years of the conflict in Palestine, the Land of Israel.

This breakthrough, in general, is the result of a simple notion: There is no better alternative than reconciliation and peace.

This lesson has to be studied by the forty-three nations and states involved in violent ethnic, religious, and national conflicts all over the globe.

On 1 October, in Washington D.C., forty-six countries and international organizations assembled at an international donors' conference to support Middle East peace. The conference mobilized resources for social and economic development in the West Bank and Gaza Strip. Among the participants were eight Arab representatives: Jordan, Egypt, Morocco, Tunisia, Saudi Arabia, Kuwait, Yemen and the PLO.

The conference pledged $2.0 billion over five years. Out of this, $600 million is earmarked for the first year and $400 million is designated for the second. In addition, the World Bank expressed its willingness to provide $450 million in loans for investments in the Territories.

The conference sent a message to the Middle East: The world is ready to lend a hand so that the peace process will be sustainable. The donors' financial support ensures that the agreement will stand firmly on two legs, one political and one social and economic.

We have learned from prior experience that political progress alone is not enough. Many Algerians sacrificed their lives to achieve independence. And although it was achieved, Algeria now faces economic depression and social upheaval. Unemployment is high. Radicalism is prevailing. Women don't enjoy equal rights. And the people resent the so-called independent political regime. This lesson must be studied.

In the words of Albert Einstein, "An empty stomach is not a good political adviser." Islamic fundamentalists who are committed to stopping the peace process, find their support among the poor—not the affluent. Poverty and the radicalism it breeds are the greatest enemies of peace.

Is it a coincidence that the Islamic fundamentalist Hamas is centered in Gaza and not in the West Bank? I don't think so. Just look at the numbers. The economy of the West Bank is twice as strong as Gaza's. We must promote the moderate, pro-peace forces in the Palestinian camp.

On 6 October, in Cairo, the Prime Minister of Israel and the Chairman of the P.L.O. met and decided to establish four joint implementation committees. This includes a committee for economic cooperation at the ministerial level. In addition, the Liaison and the Gaza-Jericho Committees already met on 13 October in Cairo and in Taba on the Red Sea.

In the meantime, Israel and Jordan agreed to establish a trilateral US-Israeli-Jordanian working group that will explore opportunities for economic development and cooperation between Israel and Jordan.

Shortly after these developments, the Prime Minister and Minister of Foreign Affairs of Israel visited Morocco. The Prime Minister paid a visit to the largest Muslim country, Indonesia. And at the UN headquarters in New York, Israel established diplomatic relations with five more states.

At the same time, the multilateral negotiations are addressing the great potentials for regional cooperation and economic growth in a peaceful Middle East. Five groups are working continuously, addressing matters of economic development, water resources, environment, refugees, and arms control and security. Israel and twelve Arab countries are taking part in these negotiations. And delegations from the European Community, Canada, Japan, China, the US, Russia, and the United Nations are active in them as well.

The progress made can be regarded as a great victory for the future-oriented over the past-oriented in the Middle East.

We still face obstacles and hardships on the way to comprehensive peace: Islamic fundamentalism, radicalism, and the proliferation of weapons of mass destruction still confront us. But I am quite confident that we shall fulfill our dream of peace and a better future.

I believe that the breakthrough that was achieved will be followed by a gradual move toward normalization and peace with other Arab countries and will create a new and promising environment in the region.

A peaceful environment will enable all countries in the Middle East to divert their human energies and economic resources away from conflict and toward better education, health, human progress, science, technology, and economic development. Our standard of living will rise and our quality of life will improve.

Paul Kennedy wrote in his book *The Rise and Fall of the Great Powers* that empires that maintained burdensome defense budgets and continued military involvement, stagnated economically and socially. They became second-rate societies.

A peaceful environment in the Middle East could free about $30 billion annually from defense budgets. (The total cost of defense in our region is about $70 billion.) This money could then be used to finance human progress and economic development rather than arms and belligerency.

Peace and stability will not only save money, but also generate growth. Less reserve duty will make our workforce more productive. Shifts from military to civilian expenditures will increase consumer demand. And the threat of war will no longer deter foreign investment and tourism.

There is no other solution but genuine cooperation in our region. This will include lowering of economic barriers, as Europe has done and as the NAFTA countries will do.

- Through regional cooperation, we have to establish a Middle Eastern Common Market.
- Through regional cooperation, we can establish an integrated network of infrastructure, including ports, airports, railways, and energy plants.

  Why should Israel and Jordan separately develop and maintain deep water seaports and modern airports on the tiny sliver of land where Eilat and Aqaba meet on the Red Sea? We can and should develop them jointly.

  We can build a railway that will connect the Gulf of Aqaba and the Mediterranean and will become an inland bridge, an alternative to the Suez Canal.

Why shouldn't we have a railway network that will go from Egypt through Israel to Lebanon, Turkey and Europe? Peace opens these options immediately.

- Through regional cooperation, we can open borders for tourism. Nature and history have endowed our region with many wondrous attractions: the sacred eternity of Jerusalem, the magnificence of the pyramids, the red palaces of Petra, the calm serenity of the Sea of Galilee, the beauty and healing powers of the Dead Sea, the holiness of Nazareth and Bethlehem, and the thrill of the ski slopes of Lebanon.
  Think of our climate, too—blue skies and summery weather. This can attract tourists from around the world. Not only can open tourism create hundreds of thousands of jobs, but also the built-in interests to preserve tranquility and peace.

- Through regional cooperation, we can promote teamwork in the fields of health, professional training, knowledge, technology, and agriculture.

- Through regional cooperation, we can launch joint ventures based on integrated knowledge, capital, and mineral resources.

- Regional cooperation will allow us to do all these things and more if we remove all types of boycotts. These boycotts handicap not only Israel, but also all societies in the region. With fully open economies, peace will bring prosperity.

To take advantage of this peace dividend, we will have to make a concerted effort to reduce expenditures on overblown arms races and inflated security forces. This will be done only when we recognize that modern economies and open societies are the partners of a democratic political system—a system run by the people and for the people.

We have chosen our path. I hope that all other nations in the Middle East will join us on the promising road to peace, growth, and a better future.

I wish that the first step we took will inspire others embroiled in conflict, to work together for reconciliation, prosperity, and peace.

Excerpted from a speech delivered to the Thirty-First Congress of the International Chamber of Commerce, in Cancun, Mexico, on 21 October 1993.

The Situation in the Middle East: United Nations 1993

After more than forty years of the Cold War and polarization, the people of the world are striving to build a better future, trying to overcome ethnic, religious, and national conflicts.

In Eastern Europe and the former Soviet Union, young democracies are struggling to lay the cornerstones of peaceful and prosperous futures.

In Western Europe, the European Union has drafted a plan of great vision. Together, these countries are building prosperous lives on the solid basis of regional cooperation.

In the Middle East too, historic changes are breaking down the battlements of a century of conflict and war. As we look forward to an era of prosperity and cooperation, I think back to a time when Jews and Arabs flourished together—one thousand years ago, in Spain, when we shared a Golden Age.

Now, the time has come for us to seize the opportunity to create a new Golden Age; to enjoy the right to our own lives and destinies. Now, it is time to lay the foundations for peace, stability, security, economic progress, and human advancement in the embattled Middle East.

We broke ground fourteen years ago, with the Camp David Accords—the first peace treaty between Israel and an Arab state.

This year, on 13 September, on the same table upon which we sealed these Accords, we signed the Declaration of Principles between Israel and the PLO.

And on 14 September, Israel and Jordan signed an agenda for negotiations toward a peace treaty.

We thank the United States for the constructive role it has played in all these achievements. And we thank the Russian Federation, Norway, and all the others whose support has helped encourage these developments.

These political breakthroughs must be accompanied by economic growth and development in order to build a stable peace. Economic and human progress are twin pillars that will support the political achievements.

Israel and the Palestinians are facing opposition, but we believe that those who look to the future will prevail over those who are trapped in the past. We both focus now on implementing the Declaration of Principles. Together, our coordinating committees are hammering out the details of implementation according to the agreed timetable.

We are making progress with the Palestinians and thirteen other Arab delegations in multilateral negotiations as well. Through these negotiations we are creating opportunities for regional cooperation.

Forty-seven countries and international organizations, including the United Nations, are participating in the multilateral talks. Five working groups are discussing refugees, arms control, regional economic cooperation, water, and the environment. Alone, each country can do little about these issues. But together, we can make great progress.

For the first time, all states participating in the talks on regional economic development agreed on a plan of action. In this plan, thirty-five projects, workshops, and studies in diverse areas will be started.

For the first time in the multilateral negotiations, talks about the Middle East, among the countries of the Middle East, are being held in the Middle East. Egypt hosted the environment working group in mid-November, and Tunisia welcomed the group on refugees a month earlier. And in April 1994, the working group on water is scheduled to convene in Oman.

For the first time, we are seeing true breakthroughs in both the bilateral and multilateral realms. But our work is not close to complete. The peace process would be greatly helped by a summit in Damascus or Jerusalem between President Assad of Syria and Prime Minister Rabin of Israel. Let us create another psychological and political breakthrough, as Egyptian President Sadat did, when he came to Jerusalem in November 1977.

Let us enjoy a quiet, secure border with Lebanon. Israel has no territorial claims in Lebanon. We look forward to a peace treaty and hope that the Lebanese government will assert its sovereignty and disarm the terrorists who use its land as a base for attacks on Israel.

We also call upon King Hussein of Jordan to sign a peace treaty with Israel. As Israeli Foreign Minister Shimon Peres said in this hall, "We live side by side with the Jordanian Kingdom, and what is so obvious geographically must become clear politically." A treaty would be the capstone on the advancements we have already made toward peaceful relations between our countries.

We desire a comprehensive peace, based on individual treaties with the Gulf States, the North African States, and all other Arab and Muslim countries.

I wish to express my regret over the expressions of violence, the injuries and the loss of human life, and over the absence of restraint and tolerance, despite the opening of new horizons before us all. I believe that this difficult period will pass. I believe that all sides know that we have crossed the point of no return on our way to a new era of peace, security, and economic and social progress.

During yesterday's debate I said, "Of course, there are, and will be, ups and downs in the process; this is a time of transition. But now is the time to realize the simple truth: We can choose either painful compromise or perpetual conflict.

"The implementation will succeed if both parties work persistently, pragmatically, and professionally toward this end. I believe both sides are proceeding in this spirit, despite moments of hardship and outbreaks of violence."

Let us progress quickly, for threats to peace will grow with time. Nuclear proliferation and a spiralling arms race cast long shadows over the Middle East. And dangerous Muslim fanatics threaten to bring a dark age to the region.

Iranian-backed groups such as Hizballah, Hamas, and the Islamic Jihad have targeted the peace process and its Arab and Israeli supporters. This is part of their broad strategy to destabilize the entire region and fulfill their dreams of expansion and domination.

When we signed the Declaration of Principles with the PLO and the world welcomed our progress with a shower of blessings and warm wishes, the fanatics responded with a hail of threats and violence.

Together with all responsible, moderate forces in the Middle East, who seek a better future, we shall fight terror with all our might, and we shall pursue peace with all our resolve.

Albert Einstein once said, "The world is a dangerous place to live—not because of the people who are evil, but because of the people who don't do anything about it."

It is time that the United Nations support the peacemakers by adopting an attitude that reflects the changes in the Middle East. When bitter enemies take bold steps toward reconciliation, the United Nations must give its support and encouragement.

We and the Palestinians have together chosen our road to peace. And we ask the United Nations to support this choice.

It is time to remove from the agenda resolutions that contradict the Declaration of Principles. It is time to abandon obsolete, anachronistic resolutions that don't reflect the new realities in the Middle East. Resolutions wielded as political weapons at the height of the Arab-Israel conflict have no place in this era of negotiation and reconciliation.

In their place let us adopt resolutions that contribute to peace and demonstrate that the United Nations will rise to the challenges and opportunities of a changing world. I am pleased that a new resolution was tabled yesterday by the United States and Russia supporting the peace process and its achievements and calling for international assistance, regional cooperation, and a comprehensive peace.

Four Israeli soldiers remain missing in action: Tzvi Feldman, Zechariah Baumel, Yehuda Katz, and Ron Arad. We call upon those countries and organizations holding them to abide by international law, display humanitarian sensitivity, and bring them home.

We also call upon our negotiating partners to lay down economic weapons and end the Arab boycott. The boycott can never be accepted and certainly not when we are advancing peace. The boycott is an obstacle to peace that impedes prosperity and hurts all societies in the Middle East.

Arabs and Israelis should profit from economic cooperation, not suffer from economic warfare. Let us unite to create a better future—a future of peace and security, economic growth, and social advancement.

Israelis and Arabs should prosper together, through cooperation. Indeed, with the Copenhagen Action Plan agreed to in November, we have already begun. We can integrate our infrastructure: seaports and airports, roads and railways, electricity grids and energy plants.

Cairo, Jerusalem, Amman, Beirut, Damascus—all were joined by road and rail before 1948. We will renew these links, and we will create new ones. Commercial trucks will stream across borders on new highways. Tourists will flow from country to country on commercial flights and modern trains.

And in Eilat, Aqaba, Gaza, and Ashkelon—we can build free trade zones that draw investment and create jobs. Israel and Jordan should jointly develop and maintain one deep water seaport and one modern airport on the tiny strip where Eilat and Aqaba meet on the Red Sea. A new railway will become an overland bridge connecting the port in the Gulf of Eilat with ships in the Mediterranean Sea.

Open borders for tourism will bridge the gulf of understanding and create the economic interests to preserve tranquility and peace. Nature and history have endowed our region with many wondrous attractions. Pilgrims of three religions seek their spiritual roots in Hebron, Jerusalem, Bethlehem, and Mecca. Vacationers flock to Tel Aviv and Sharm-a-Sheikh for beautiful beaches under blue skies and balmy weather. And travelers marvel at the incredible sights of Luxor, Petra, Baalbek, and Timna.

Cooperation in tourism will generate hundreds of thousands of jobs, strengthen our economies, and fortify peace.

We will reap great benefits if we sow the seeds of peace and cooperation now. Speaking at a dinner in honor of Israel's Prime Minister Yitzhak Rabin, the Secretary-General of the United Nations said, "Now there is a new moment in time. . . . We have seen that negotiations can work. . . . We have seen a small seed of trust start to take root."

We still face difficulties as we make the agreement a reality. The enemies of peace are trying to prevent our success. But we will continue striving to achieve a comprehensive peace in the Middle East. Peace is the foundation of security, regional cooperation, economic development, and personal advancement.

This is our obligation to future generations—to the young, to our children. This is our obligation to ourselves, to our moral convictions. This is our obligation to the nations and people we represent.

Let the international community represented here work in the same spirit, with the same sense of obligation and with the same dedication to this great goal.

Excerpted from a speech delivered in the United Nations General Assembly, 1 December 1993.

Opening Doors

At the outset, I cannot but refer to the tragic massacre that occurred in Tel Aviv yesterday. Twenty-two people were killed and forty-eight injured by the terrorists from Hamas, an Islamic fundamentalist group.

The attack on the bus followed two other murderous terrorist incidents that took place in Jerusalem last week. These fanatics seek to kill the peace process by murdering innocent civilians, in contravention of all human values and international norms.

But even if we are still in shock and in a period of mourning, I would like to stress that Israel will not allow terrorist acts such as these to weaken its commitment to peace.

This is a watershed in the history of the Middle East. The changes we are taking part in are creating the opportunity to reshape the future of the entire region and its people.

I believe that the mutual recognition between Israel and the Palestinians paved the way for the peace treaty between Israel and Jordan that will be signed next week. Similarly, without the initial agreement with Jordan in July, there would be no agreement with Morocco, no agreement with Tunisia, and no declaration by the Gulf States ending the secondary and tertiary economic boycott of Israel. None of this could have been achieved without the peace that has existed between Israel and Egypt since 1979.

****

The Israeli-Jordanian peace treaty is a major step toward comprehensive peace in our region, but its main importance is first and foremost for the two peoples. The treaty's economic impact will be felt immediately, especially in the area of tourism. Next week, the doors will be opened, and tourists will flow freely back and forth. Later on, the impact will be felt in many other spheres.

On the Israeli-Palestinian track, we have seen three major implementation agreements since the DOP was signed one year ago: We signed the Protocol on Economic Relations that makes possible an open economic relationship between Israel and the Palestinians. The Gaza-Jericho Agreement has begun the implementation of the DOP in the Gaza Strip and Jericho area and allowed the Israel Defense Forces to complete their redeployment in those areas. On 29 August, the Early Empowerment agreement was signed to transfer responsibility for education and culture, tourism, health, welfare, and taxation to the Palestinians.

To fully implement the agreements, the Palestinian Authority (P.A.) will need funding. Two billion dollars was pledged last October by forty-six countries and organizations. Although the donors commonly restrict their giving to specific projects, they showed flexibility by donating funds to support general Palestinian administrative costs.

****

Much attention has focused on economic support for the peace process. We have learned from previous experience that political progress alone is not enough.

Islamic fundamentalist extremists who are committed to stopping the peace process find their support among the poor—not the affluent. Poverty and the radicalism it breeds are the greatest enemies of making real progress toward peace.

The people of the Middle East have a window of opportunity that won't stay open forever. Today, the world is focused on the Middle East. But attention spans can be short. This is the *raison d'etre* of the Casablanca Conference that will take place on 30 October. Board-level executives from over nine hundred companies and high-ranking government officials from approximately seventy countries, including heads of state and ministers, are expected to be in attendance.

The Conference will attempt to lay the economic foundations of a lasting peace through regional cooperation. Interactive working sessions will focus on specific areas such as information technology, the Palestinian economy, and regional trade and exports.

For governments, it will be a forum to promote their ideas for economic growth. For businesses, it will be an opportunity to forge ties and to examine possibilities for investment and joint ventures. Israel will be furnishing compilations of ongoing and proposed projects in such areas as tourism, transportation, communications, energy, agriculture, water, the environment, and human resource development.

* * * * * * * * *

I believe there is no other solution but genuine cooperation in our region.

One area where sizable investment will be involved is the water sector. It is impossible to overemphasize the importance of working together to solve the problem of water scarcity. Instead of disagreeing on how to divide up existing resources, we should be agreeing on ways to expand all our sources of water. (This approach became a part of the peace treaty between Israel and Jordan.)

Regional cooperation will allow us to do all this and much more if all types of boycotts are removed. These are economic weapons whose main casualties are the people and their well-being. We are glad that the Gulf States decided to remove the secondary and tertiary boycotts, and we hope that many more Arab states will do the same very soon.

* * * * * * * * *

All of the different possibilities for regional cooperation and development are interrelated. Allow me to illustrate with some possibilities for regional cooperation. In light of the new peace treaty, I will focus my remarks on Israeli-Jordanian cooperation as a case in point.

There is great potential for cooperation in developing the Dead Sea area—both for tourism and for exploitation of its mineral resources. We are studying opportunities for cooperation in digging a canal from the Red Sea to the Dead Sea. The steep drop in altitude would allow us to generate large amounts of electricity and to desalinate water. The remaining water that would flow into the Dead Sea would reverse the evaporation that has dried up much of its southern half.

We have already agreed with the Jordanians and Americans to work on preparing a master plan for the Jordan Rift Valley to encourage investment and project development there.

- Israeli and Jordanian experience has demonstrated the valley's potential for agricultural productivity, especially for out-of-season produce in the European markets.
- We have agreed on the establishment of an Eilat/Aqaba Free Tourism Zone. The potential for tourism in the area is great, and the area lends itself to joint development of sites blending the arid desert climate with water-based recreational facilities. The variety of marine life in the Gulf of Aqaba can also serve as a draw to tourists and a basis for cooperation.
- In two meetings this month, one in Israel and one in Jordan, we are exploring creating a Free Trade Zone in Eilat and Aqaba, based on the principle of free flow of goods between countries.

I believe that, in the long run, the key to economic development lies in the creation and expansion of such a free trade zone to include Israel, Jordan, the Palestinians and other countries.

****

What is important for a country's economic and human development are geopolitical factors (such as peace or war), scientific, technological and human factors, and the degree of integration in the global economy and trade and in the world information system.

Israel's foreign trade ties her primarily with the European Economic Community, the United States, and the Far East. But it would be most natural to develop economic and commercial ties with our neighbors. I am aware that some voices in the Arab countries have expressed concern that Israel's economy would be so strong as to dominate the other economies. But let me assure them, we are interested in cooperation—not domination. We know that there is a connection between the economic and human situation and the chances for reconciliation and peace, which is our principal goal. A high standard of living for all people in the region is our best guarantee of peace and stability.

I believe that we have reached the end of the beginning of the Arab-Israeli peace process. But the most important work still lies ahead of us—to translate words into reality. Without an active struggle against terrorism and fanaticism, and without a change in the social, economic, and human conditions, we will be unable to create a long term political change.

All sides bear a huge responsibility. Much can be lost. Even more can be gained.

Excerpted from a speech delivered on 20 October 1994, to a UN Conference on Trade and Development-sponsored symposium on trade efficiency.

The Situation in the Middle East: United Nations 1994

Far-reaching changes are reshaping the Middle East. The speed and extent of this transformation are unmatched in the world today.

Israel and its neighbors have established relations through various tracks of the peace process: with the Palestinians, with Jordan, and with states of the Persian Gulf and North Africa. The multilateral negotiations are bearing fruit as a framework for regional cooperation. We continue to look forward to progress with Syria and Lebanon.

The economic summit that recently convened in Casablanca, Morocco reflected the desire of countries in the region to establish economic cooperation between them. There was consensus among the conference participants that boycotts are incompatible with this goal. As was stated in the Casablanca Declaration: "The participants . . . explored how best to accelerate the development of the region and overcome, as soon as possible, obstacles, including boycotts and all barriers to trade and investment. All agreed that there is a need to promote increased investment from inside and outside the region. They noted that such investment requires free movement of goods, capital, and labor across borders in accordance with market forces, technical cooperation based on mutual interest, openness to the international economy, and appropriate institutions to promote economic interaction. . . . In this context, the participants noted favorably the decision of the Council for the Cooperation of the Gulf States regarding the lifting of the secondary and the tertiary aspects of the boycott of Israel." The boycott is an obsolete economic weapon whose main casualty is regional prosperity. We hope soon to see it abolished in its entirety.

The Casablanca Conference ensured that both the public and private sectors would have a voice in shaping new economic arrangements for the region. Representatives of sixty governments and the Palestinian Authority participated in the Summit. They were joined by over eleven hundred business leaders from around the world, including hundreds of Israelis and Arabs. The Casablanca Conference broke down walls of mistrust. In their place it cemented the foundations of economic cooperation in the Middle East. Arab and Israeli businessmen met each other face to face. They exchanged ideas and discussed proposals.

All these developments represent a dramatic turning point for the Middle East, for the relations between Israel and her neighbors, and for the creation of a better future that all people of the region can enjoy.

We are witnessing important steps toward peace. But at the same time, we see an opposing trend towards radicalization, fanaticism, and violence. It imperils the entire region.

Today we witnessed yet another act of terrorism against innocent Israeli citizens. A terrorist, affiliated with Hamas, and armed with an ax, brutally murdered a young woman in northern Israel several hours ago. Liat Gabai died of her wounds on the way to the hospital. She was nineteen years old.

Radical fundamentalist organizations threaten the stability of governments and states, terrorizing innocents without distinction. Hamas, Islamic Jihad, and Hizballah have raised the cry of "jihad," holy war, against all so-called infidels. They, together with similar organizations, are active in every corner of the Middle East and beyond: in Algeria, Sudan, Egypt, Morocco, Tunisia, Jordan, Syria, Lebanon, in the areas controlled by the Palestinian Authority, in Israel, and even in Argentina, the United Kingdom, and the United States. Their primary goal is to establish a radical religious empire, in their own words, "From the Atlantic Ocean to China."

In the meantime, they focus on the elimination of peace. For this, they enlist financial support from backers in the United States, Europe, and other places. But they rely primarily on Iran. Yet even though this fact is well known, many countries still maintain elaborate ties with the Iranian regime, including the sale of arms and other military equipment, as well as technological, economic, and financial assistance.

Will the region move toward peace and cooperation, as the peacemakers desire? Or will it be drawn backward into the shadows of conflict and bloodshed, as promised by the radical fundamentalists? Political agreements are the first steps to ensure peace. Then all peoples of the region must be able to enjoy the great social and economic potentials it offers.

The dream of regional cooperation is steadily becoming a reality. Having signed a peace treaty with Jordan, we are now seeking to bring the benefits of peace to both peoples. We are working with Jordan to find ways of jointly developing shared resources.

The opportunities are enormous: Exploitation of mineral resources in the Dead Sea, agricultural development in the Arava valley, and integration of infrastructures in the sister cities of Eilat and Aqaba, which meet on the Red Sea. As a first step, we have begun work on linking electricity grids in certain areas, saving money, and increasing efficiency.

Israel and Jordan have also agreed to establish an Eilat/Aqaba Free Tourism Zone. The area lends itself to joint development of sites blending the arid desert climate with water-based recreational facilities and the natural wonders of the Gulf of Aqaba. Development of the region for tourism could serve as a basis for cooperation between Israel, Jordan, Egypt, and eventually Saudi Arabia. The inspiring contrast of red desert mountains, pale blue skies, and indigo waters could make the Red Sea riviera a favorite escape for vacationers from around the world.

In Eilat and Aqaba, Israel and Jordan are also exploring the creation of a free trade zone, based on the principle of free flow of goods between countries. Such a free trade zone could eventually be expanded to include all of Israel, Jordan, the Palestinian Authority, and nearby countries.

Progress is also being made in the multilateral negotiations. These talks bring together Israel and many other countries in the Middle East to encourage regional cooperation in four fields: environmental protection, development of water resources, economic cooperation, arms control and regional security, and refugees.

The road before us is long, but our destination is clear: peace and reconciliation, cooperation and prosperity. This is the key to a better future for the people of the Middle East. It is the only key to ending the suffering and loss of human life. It is the key to a new hope in the hearts of all.

The international community bears a solemn responsibility: to assist in bringing about this profound change. It can do this by supporting the states and parties that are turning toward the future and by stopping those who would destroy the great opportunity that has opened before us.

This is a historic opportunity and a momentous challenge. May we all rise to the occasion.

Excerpted from a speech delivered in the United Nations General Assembly, 30 November 1994.

5

Terrorism and Fundamentalism: The Enemies of Peace

Letter to Secretary-General of the United Nations

I wish to convey the deep concern of the government and people of Israel following the extensive racist, anti-Semitic, and xenophobic outbursts that have taken place recently in many countries. The flames set by racists and bigots recall memories of the horrible inferno of Nazism, which consumed the lives of tens of millions from many nations and destroyed one-third of the Jewish people

Recently, there has been a wave of violent manifestations of racism and anti-Semitism. Hate crimes have targeted refugees, asylum seekers, foreigners, and others. In 1990, there were 46 violent attacks against Jews, while in 1991 there were 61 attacks. Thus far in 1992, there have been close to 100 such incidents, in addition to some 250 cases of threats, arson, and damage to property. Across Europe, there are currently more than one thousand organizations with an anti-Semitic orientation.

The government of Israel, headed by the Prime Minster, Mr. Yitzhak Rabin, discussed the racist and anti-Semitic phenomena at its weekly cabinet meeting on 29 November 1992. The government then issued a communique that stated, inter alia, that it "strongly condemns" the recent neo-Nazi, racist, and anti-Semitic phenomena and "views them with concern and seriousness . . . the cabinet will continue to be active in the monitoring of anti-Semitic phenomena everywhere, and in the struggle there against, as needs and circumstances require."

The president of Israel, Mr. Chaim Herzog, has appealed to the leaders and heads of state of a number of countries suggesting the issuance of a joint condemnation of racism and anti-Semitism.

In the Knesset, on 30 November 1992, Mr. Shimon Peres, Israel's minister of foreign affairs, stated that, "so long as such manifestations continue, we cannot rest. We cannot lower our voices. The government of Israel shall assert in a clear, unapologetic voice our demand to do everything necessary to nip this phenomenon in the bud."

It is the duty of the world to remember the atrocities of the past and not to allow them to cast their ugly shadow upon the future. Nations should enact appropriate legislation and severely punish those who commit acts of racist violence. It is our duty and our mission to condemn this threat without hesitation and to put an end to it.

Originally sent on 15 December 1992.

Hamas Deportations: Security Council 1992

The enemies of peace are on the warpath. Discouraged and dismayed by the bilateral negotiations between Israel and its Arab neighbors, terrorists organizations such as Islamic Jihad and Hamas have been mounting a relentless campaign of intimidation and bloodshed. Their goal is very simple: to kill Israelis and others and to kill the peace process.

Since 1 March 1992, the Islamic fundamentalist group Hamas has carried out thirty terrorist attacks against Israelis, which have left eleven dead and nine wounded. On 24 May 1992, a Hamas terrorist stabbed to death an Israeli teenager, Helena Rapp. Three days later, on 27 May 1992, Talmudic scholar and teacher Rabbi Shimon Biran was attacked by a Hamas terrorist who stabbed him repeatedly and killed him. More recently, on 7 December 1992, Lieutenant Hagai Amit, Sgt. Major Yehuda Zamir, and Sgt. Major Shalom Tzabari were killed by Hamas terrorists who opened fire on their jeep. A few hours later, two dozen members of Hamas paraded through Gaza City, proudly proclaiming Hamas's responsibility for the attack. On 12 December 1992, Hamas terrorists in a moving vehicle opened fire on another jeep, killing the driver, Yuval Tutanji, and injuring two other soldiers. On 15 December 1992, the body of hostage Sgt. Major Nissim Toledano was found on the Jersualem-Jericho highway. Members of Hamas had kidnapped him in his hometown of Lod and then strangled him and stabbed him to death. Those acts of barbarism were committed by those who are opposed to the peace talks. They are but further links in the chain of Hamas terror.

Islamic Jihad has a long and extensive record of terrorist attacks against Israeli soldiers and civilians. On 22 February 1992, a terrorist armed with a kitchen knife stabbed an Israeli to death and wounded three others in Kfar Sava. Islamic Jihad claimed responsibility for the attack. On 21 October 1990 an Islamic Jihad terrorist murdered three Israelis in the Baka neighborhood of Jerusalem. Indifferent to the blood they shed and the pain they cause, terrorist organizations such as Hamas and Islamic Jihad continue to wreak havoc.

The shrill polemics of the terrorists leave no doubt about their intentions. In a leaflet issued on 23 September 1991, Hamas declared its unyielding opposition to the very notion of a Middle East peace conference and called for "a serious and effective move at all levels to foil the capitulation conference. . . . " (Al-Ribat, 24 September 1991, cited in FBIS-NES-91-201). The Hamas leaflet also resorted to crude anti-Semitism when it declared, "All the Arab and Islamic peoples and movements must proceed immediately to perform their desired and expected role in the decisive fateful battle against Jews, the enemies of God and humanity.

Hamas rejects the very existence of Israel and calls for its destruction. The covenant of Hamas, which was published in August 1988, states that "The liberation of Palestine in its entirety, from the sea to the river, is the most lofty of strategic goals." Among the methods that Hamas advocates as a means of achieving that goal are the murder of Jews and the burning of their property. In leaflet number 65, which was distributed in October 1990, Hamas declared that, "every Jew is a settler and it is our obligation to kill him."

In a speech broadcast on Jordanian television on 27 November 1990, the leader of Islamic Jihad, Sheikh Assad Tamimi said, "The destiny of the Jews is to be slaughtered by us . . . we have taken it upon ourselves to do our duty to society and torture them because torture is the destiny of the Jews." In an interview with Stern magazine published on 14 February 1991, Sheikh Tamimi said, "No Jew is innocent! All Jews must be killed. They . . . have in their long history only brought misfortune to mankind." Sheikh Tamimi may not be obligated to acknowledge that the Bible was given to the world by the Jewish people, or that Moses, Freud, Kafka, and Einstein were all Jews. But the enlightened world is obligated to give Sheikh Tamimi what he deserves.

Hamas and Islamic Jihad have engaged in operations that have included gunfire attacks on Israeli civilians and soldiers, the murder of suspected Palestinian collaborators, kidnappings, and hostage takings. And yet, despite the violent attacks against Israelis, despite the hateful and anti-Semitic rhetoric, some member states of this council are willing to criticize Israel for protecting its citizens and for taking measures in self-defense.

Surely the members of the Council are aware of the legitimate actions taken recently by other governments in the region in the face of violence and threats by Islamic fundamentalist terrorist groups directed against the people and authorities in those states. The members of the council are certainly aware as well of the threats against other governments from fanatical groups of Islamic fundamentalists that might threaten the stability of those countries. Ignoring the serious threats posed by extremist groups may only endanger the stability of the Middle East and the prospects for reconciliation.

The government of Israel, headed by Prime Minster Yitzhak Rabin, will take whatever steps it deems necessary in order to protect the people of Israel. We can not allow terrorist groups such as Hamas and Islamic Jihad to murder with impunity. No government in the world would stand by idly in the face of persistent terrorist attacks against its citizenry, and neither shall we. The right of self-defense is the natural right of any nation and state. We are determined to fight the forces of terrorism and to defend ourselves.

Since December 1987, at least 809 Palestinians have been murdered by Palestinian terrorists in the territories. Such acts of murder and extremism cannot be allowed to go unpunished, for doing so only creates more violence and encourages further extremism and fanaticism.

Israel did not give in when terrorists took Israeli students hostage at Maalot. Israel did not give in when terrorists took hostages at the Savoy Hotel in Tel Aviv. Israel did not give in when terrorists took hostages to Entebbe. And Israel shall not give in to the terrorists of Islamic Jihad and Hamas, who have murdered innocent people, kidnapped Israelis, and want to kidnap the peace process from the people of the Middle East.

Therefore, Israel has decided to remove, for a period that will not extend beyond two years, members of terrorist organizations whose actions endanger the lives of people or who incite others to such actions. Israel has issued temporary removal orders against hundreds of members of the terrorist organizations Hamas and Islamic Jihad, including their political and military leaders. This measure of temporary removal is consistent with the instructions of international and Israeli law. After carefully examining the relevant legal issues for fourteen hours, the Supreme Court of Israel allowed the temporary removal measures to proceed. While Nissim Toledano and other Jewish and Palestinian victims of the terrorists have no ability to appeal or protest, the terrorists themselves are being granted such a right through authorized Committees of Appeals.

I believe that the majority of people in the Middle East—Arabs, Jews, and others—are hoping to depart from the path of conflict and violence and are seeking to shape a new relationship and a better future for the peoples of the region based on reconciliation and peace. Israel remains fully committed to the quest for peace. We shall not withdraw from the peace talks in Washington, D.C. We shall not allow Hamas, Islamic Jihad, and others to undermine the peacemaking process. Prime Minister Rabin stated at a special Knesset session on 15 December 1992, "We have only one course, and it is a dual one: a search for peace, and an uncompromising war on terrorism. Despite the pain, we continue to cling to the pursuit of peace." In an announcement issued on 17 December 1992, Israel declared that

> The Government has determined that it is fully committed to making peace and it is its intention to continue the negotiations being currently held in Washington. The government views peace as the central objective of its policies. In parallel to the peace making, the Government is determined to fight terror in all its forms, and will strike at those who harm the citizens of Israel and the peace making.

We remain firm in our hope that the current set of negotiations will yield fruitful results, and we call upon our neighbors to continue with the negotiations.

The Palestinians may now make yet another great mistake by choosing to desert the negotiations. They made a historic mistake, from their point of view, in 1948, when they rejected the Partition Plan. They made another mistake when they rejected the Camp David Accords. And now, they may give in to Hamas and Islamic Jihad, sacrificing their future in the process. Such a great mistake would serve to reconfirm the remark of Ambassador Abba Eban that the Palestinians never miss an opportunity to miss an opportunity.

On 17 December 1992, the White House issued a statement, and I fully concur with its assertion that

> Peace between Israel and its neighbors has never been more achievable. A way has been created whereby the people of the Middle East

can escape the wars that have too often defined the region's history. Making peace a reality through these negotiations is the only way to frustrate those who would sabotage the peace process by violence.

I have not come here today to sit as a defendant in the dock. Rather, I am here on behalf of the people of Israel as an accuser of the forces of terrorism, who seek to harm the moral foundations of civilized society. I am here as an accuser of those who so cruelly target the innocent to further their fanatical goals. I am here as an accuser of those who are trying, at any price and in any way possible, to murder the prospects for peace.

It is time for this council to cease condemning the victims of terrorism. The enemies of peace are using terrorism to try to divert us all away from the path toward peace. We must not allow them to succeed. There is simply too much at stake for the future of all of us.

Excerpted from a speech delivered in the United Nations Security Council, 18 December 1992.

The Middle East Arms Race

Recent developments in the Middle East can be assessed both with apprehension and hope; there is bad news and good news.

First, I would like to address the worrisome developments in the field of arms proliferation in the Middle East; then present the encouraging developments in the peacemaking process between Israel and several of its Arab neighbors, and finally, assess very briefly the overall situation.

Perhaps the two most discouraging developments are Iran's race to become a nuclear power and Iraq's continuing evasion, even under a comprehensive inspection regime, from fully complying with the requirement to eliminate its weapons of mass destruction.

In recent years, Iran has embarked on a campaign to become the regional power in the Gulf. Using Iraq's defeat in the Gulf War and its growing oil revenues, Iran has launched a massive arms procurement program, purchasing tanks, missiles, submarines, and other military hardware.

However, the most worrisome development is Iran's attempt to become a nuclear power. Telltale signs of work on a military nuclear program have been reported in the Western press, such as the existence of several nuclear centers, trained manpower, and huge investments in purchasing relevant equipment and technology, especially from China and several Western countries.

It is true that Iran has signed the Non-Proliferation Treaty (NPT), but so did Iraq. NPT does not seem to be the right answer to proliferation in the Middle East. Iran's blatant threats against Israel and its massive support for the Hizbullah terror organization in Lebanon should serve as a warning signal to all of us. The West should not make the same mistake with Iran as it did with Iraq.

The second worrisome development is Iraq's remaining nonconventional threat. Although a primary part of its nuclear program and of its chemical weapons stockpile were destroyed during the Gulf War and by UN and IAEA inspection teams afterward, Iraq, under Saddam Hussein, continues to play games with UN inspections. Moreover, Iraq has quite remarkably reconstructed its conventional military forces. No on can be certain that Iraq is not hiding hundreds of SCUD missiles, biological-warfare capabilities, and nuclear materials. The most prominent threat is the indisputable ability of Iraq to continue its nuclear program once the inspection regime is lifted. Nobody can take from Iraq its know-how and its trained personnel (thousands of scientists and technicians in the nuclear field).

Third, there exists the threat of leakage of nuclear material, sophisticated technologies and know-how and nuclear experts and technicians from the republics of the former Soviet Union to the Middle East. The dismantlement of the Soviet Union and the economic chaos that followed enhance the chances of this threat materializing.

Last but not least, and maybe the most dangerous development in the short-run, is the spiraling arms race that is taking place in the region. While Israel had to cut its military order of battle several times in recent years due to economic constraints, the Arabs and especially Syria, Saudi Arabia, Iran, and the Gulf states have been purchasing large quantities of modern tanks, state-of-the-art fighters, and long-range missiles, practically covering the whole area of Israel.

This fearful influx of modern weapons into the Middle East, coming in large part from the West, clearly destabilizes the already volatile situation and augments the potential of deterioration into violent conflicts. So far, initiatives to curb the arms race have not succeeded.

In the multilateral talks, notable progress has been made in the working-group (WG) of Regional Security and Arms Control (RS & AC).

First, the fact that several Arab states are discussing with Israel RS & AC issues is outstanding by itself. The Middle East as you all know, has been more active in the arms race than in arms control.

Second, the participants had the chance to get familiar with each other, to learn, through joint seminars, from others experience in this field (especially, U.S. & Russian experience) and to come to terms with the right track to advance in this WG. After the initial opening meeting in Moscow in 1991 and two working seminars in Washington (May 1992) and Moscow (September 1992), the third meeting is scheduled for early this year. There is an understanding among the participants that the practical track to proceed in this area is by establishing confidence-building measures and by practicing them a long time. Only after basic confidence is established, and hopefully getting encouragement from positive developments in the bilateral peace talks, may one arrive at negotiations on arms control. This was the way security and arms control agreements have been negotiated and achieved in Europe (the Helsinki process) and between the Superpowers. One cannot really expect the volatile region of the Middle East to jump immediately to the field of disarmament, as the Arabs are pressing for. Let us not forget that several of the main actors in the Middle East are not participating yet in the discussions of the RS & AC WG (to mention only Syria, Lebanon, Iran, Iraq, and Libya, as examples).

We believe that the step-by-step approach in this field is the only possible way to advance, given the special and delicate strategic position of Israel, on the one hand, and the historical record of the field of arms control, on the other.

With your permission I would like now to wrap up this part of my presentation with several concluding remarks.

First, in the overall assessment I am optimistic. Once there is a breakthrough in the peacemaking process, it will have considerable positive ramifications on the stability and security of the region, and it will probably boost the negotiations in the multilateral track.

Second, a more comprehensive effort is needed in the Middle East, where, following the Iraqi experience, the international community will have to do the following:

a. Continue to monitor Iraq very closely, in order to prevent its reemergence as a nuclear threat to the region and to Israel.
b. Keep a close watch over Iran and its efforts to become a nuclear power and prevent such a fearful development by blocking any nuclear related or dual-use equipment and tech-

nology from arriving in Iran and by applying other appropriate measures.

c. Encourage Israel in its bold political initiatives for peace by helping to improve its economy; by providing it with what is required to maintain the qualitative edge over its adversaries in the very troublesome balance of forces prevailing now in the region, and by not pressing it to accept disarmament initiatives imposed from the outside. The only way for Israel to proceed in this area is through free and direct negotiations with its neighbors and by using the step-by-step and confidence-building approach. In this regard let me note the fact that Israel has been showing its good will and participation by sponsoring a CWC resolution in the UNGA last November and by signing the CWC in Paris on 13 January 1993, while most Arab countries failed to sign it.

d. Moderating the spiralling arms race in the Middle East, particularly by reducing the massive flow of sophisticated arms to the region and especially to Arab states.

In summary, Israel has taken bold steps toward peace in 1992. It has to be supported in all the areas mentioned above, especially by the U.S., a strong and generous ally, in order to achieve at last a just and stable peace in the Middle East.

Excerpted from a speech delivered on 11 January 1993 to the annual meeting of the B'nai B'rith International Board of Governors.

Islamic Fundamentalism: The Threat to Peace

The spread of militant Islamic fundamentalism poses a grave threat to the stability of the Middle East. The growing power of the Islamic fundamentalists, along with their uncompromising and inflexible fanaticism, endangers the entire region. The fundamentalists are using two methods to further their goals: ballots and bullets. From Jordan to Algeria to Egypt to Tunisia, Islamic fundamentalists have been striving to undermine the ruling regimes in order to establish militant theocratic states. Backed by Iran and Sudan, the fundamentalists are succeeding in spreading their influence throughout the region.

As the *New York Times* reported on 21 December 1992, "well over twenty ideological and military training camps in Sudan, Lebanon, and Iran are being run by Arabic-speaking Iranian Revolutionary Guards." The Iranian Foreign Ministry, according to the *Times* article, "has a division to manage Arab fundamentalists." With financial and spiritual support from Iran, the fundamentalists are able to carry out well-trained and well-financed operations from one end of the Arab world to the other.

- Fundamentalists in Egypt have been waging a violent campaign since March, primarily in Upper Egypt, aimed at Coptic Christians and security forces, and there have been machine gun attacks on tourists. It is worth recalling that it was militant fundamentalists who murdered President Anwar Sadat for having signed a peace treaty with Israel.
- In Algeria, the Islamic Front won 188 of the 231 seats in the first round of voting in December 1991. The second round of the elections, scheduled for January 1992, was canceled after it became clear that the fundamentalists would take control of the government. The fundamentalists are now waging an armed and violent struggle that has left at least two hundred police and army officials dead in the past year.
- In Jordan, the Muslim Brotherhood controls thirty-four of the eighty seats in Jordan's parliament, making them the biggest bloc in the legislature.
- In Kuwait, fundamentalists won nineteen of fifty seats in parliamentary elections that were held on 5 October 1992, and they subsequently received three cabinet positions in the new Kuwaiti government.
- In Sudan, a military revolution in June 1989 brought to power a fundamentalist government that has close ties to Iran and that has been accused by the Egyptian authorities of fomenting violence and unrest in neighboring states.

Spreading fundamentalism is part of Iran's drive to expand its regional power. At the same time, Iran is also engaged in a massive arms buildup. Between 1989 and 1991, Iran signed weapons contracts worth $6 billion with China and the former Soviet Union for MIG-29 planes, Sukhoi-24 Bombers, three submarines and eight hundred modern tanks. In addition, during 1991, Iran obtained some fifty–seventy SCUD missile launchers. Iran is also working very hard to develop its nuclear military capability, spending $800 million annually. It is conceivable that within 5–7 years, Iran might have nuclear weapons.

Regarding Iran's weapons purchases, the *New York Times* commented in an editorial on 16 November 1992, "In the hands of a regime that still sponsors international terrorism and exports Islamic revolution, this dramatic buildup could develop into a world-class problem."

Islamic fundamentalism poses a threat to Israel as well. The fundamentalist groups Hamas and Islamic Jihad have been waging a campaign of terror and violence aimed at murdering Israelis and others and murdering the peace process. Hamas and Islamic Jihad have been responsible for at least 157 attacks against Israelis that have killed 36 Jews and wounded 148. They have also brutally murdered at least 107 Palestinians in the territories. On 18 December 1992, the spokesman of the Israel Defense Forces announced the arrest of a member of the Islamic Jihad who had plotted to kill Palestinian leader Faisal Husseini. The terrorist had planned to kill him at a public event in Jerusalem in order to undermine the peace talks.

The continuing involvement of Hamas and Islamic Jihad in terrorist activities directed against Israelis and Palestinians further demonstrates the necessity of combating the dangerous phenomenon of militant Islamic fundamentalism. The fundamentalists will stop at nothing to try to divert Arabs and Israelis away from the peace process. The covenant of Hamas, which was issued on 18 August 1988, states emphatically that, "There is no solution for the Palestinian problem except by jihad. Initiatives, proposals and international conferences are but a waste of time, an exercise in futility."

The Hamas covenant also says, "The day of judgement will not come about until Moslems fight Jews and kill them. Then, the Jews will hide behind rocks and trees, and the rocks and trees will cry out: 'O Moslem, there is a Jew hiding behind me, come and kill him.'"

Hamas and Islamic Jihad also view the West as their enemy. On 18 January 1991, Sheikh Nader Tamimi, the spokesman for Islamic Jihad and the son of its founder, threatened to carry out terrorist attacks against the Western countries that had joined the coalition against Iraq's invasion of Kuwait. Sheikh Tamimi said, "We now want to attack all Western countries participating in the aggression against Iraq (Reuters, 28 January 1991)."

The international community must recognize the growing danger that the militant fundamentalists pose to the Middle East. Their list of enemies is long, and it includes Israel, the West, and many Arab regimes. The world must confront this burgeoning threat if it wishes to ensure future peace and tranquility in the Middle East.

Article originally published in *The Westchester Jewish Week,* 12–18 February 1993.

We Must Act Now

Following the arrest of a suspect in the bombing of the World Trade Center (front page, 5 March), one hopes that public awareness will increase regarding the danger posed by militant Islamic fundamentalism.

Radical and uncompromising Islamic fundamentalism has spread across Asia and the Middle East with alarming speed and increasing strength. Militant fundamentalists hold sway in Iran, which now provides money, arms, and inspiration to like-minded movements, as well as in the Sudan, where a fundamentalist regime is in power. Fundamentalists have significant influence in Algeria, as well as growing political and ideological strongholds in Jordan, Egypt, Lebanon, and the territories (the Hamas and Islamic Jihad movements).

The international community must recognize the growing threat posed by radical Islamic fundamentalists. Their list of enemies is long, and it includes Israel, the West, and many Arab regimes. As the alleged link of the suspect in the World Trade Center bombing to Islamic fundamentalists shows, militant Islamic fundamentalism does not stop at country borders. Indeed, Ehud Yaari asserted (Op-Ed, 17 Jan.) that Hamas's command center is now in the United States.

The free world must act to curb and fight this menacing phenomenon. We must act now, before it is too late.

Letter to the editor of the *New York Times,* published 23 March 1993.

Memorial Service for Victims of the Buenos Aires Terrorist Attack

The explosion that tore through the heart of the Argentine Jewish community tore through the heart of every Jew and, I believe, touches the heart of every decent human being. One hundred people murdered, 230 wounded, an entire community scarred.

I would like to express my sincerest condolences to the families of all those killed as well as the entire Argentine Jewish community. I wish all those wounded a speedy and complete recovery.

Beyond the enormous human loss, the attack claimed a tragic cultural toll. Literary and historical treasures housed in the AMIA building turned to ashes. One hundred years of communal archives were wiped out. The cemetery records of an entire Jewish community turned to dust.

Following the attack last Monday, Israel immediately took action. A rescue unit of the Israel Defense Forces was dispatched to the site of the bombing. Yesterday, I sent letters to the Secretary-General of the United Nations and to the president of the Security Council. The letters will become official UN documents. Allow me to share with you some of what I wrote:

> Terrorist organizations such as the one responsible for the attack in Buenos Aires, act in the name of a radical fundamentalist ideology and seek to derail the Middle East peace process. They direct their attacks against innocent human beings, solely because they happen to be Jews or Israelis, or others who are close to them. These organizations are assisted by countries that are known for their opposition to the Middle East peace process and for their support of international terrorism, first and foremost Iran.
>
> Giving in to terrorism will only encourage more violence and bloodshed. Israel calls upon the international community to cooperate in the fight against the terrorist threat posed by these radial fundamentalist organizations and their sponsors.

These letters will be sent to all the members of the Security Council and all the member states of the United Nations.

Israel is also working with Argentina to jointly investigate the attack. I can promise you that when found, the terrorists will answer for their crimes.

It appears that the same international terrorist network is responsible for killing one hundred innocent people in Buenos Aires last week; for blowing up the Israeli Embassy there two years ago and killing twenty-nine people; for setting off bombs yesterday at the Israeli Embassy in London and at an important Jewish center there; for bombing the airplane in Panama last week; for bombing the World Trade Center in New York last year; and for attacking hundreds of Israelis and Palestinians throughout recent years.

The time has come for the countries and nations of the world to declare an all out war on this insane, fanatic threat. It is a cancer in the international and human community that must be cut out.

If it is not, it will not relent in its war against peace and the peacemakers.

As we are reminded every year on Tisha B'Av, the Jewish people have known much suffering. But we have always found strength in our heritage, in our resilience, and in our hope for the future. When we end the chanting of Eicha, we do not close on a note of despair, but rather on one of hope: "Renew our days as of old."

I believe that the Jewish people and the State of Israel are stronger today, and we shall overcome.

And so, I would like to end with a note of hope. Two days ago Israel and Jordan ended the state of war that existed for forty-six years. We have come another step closer to peace. May the day soon arrive when there will be no more war; no more terror; no more violence; no more bloodshed.

As we mourn for the victims, may their memory be for a blessing to us all. Amen.

Excerpted from an address delivered on 17 July 1994 at the Fifth Avenue Synagogue in New York City.

With the commander of UNDOF, the UN peacekeeping force on the Golan Heights.

At an evening in support of Israel's Open University. With a representative of the Open University and close friends Harvey Krueger, Barbara Mandel, Morton Mandel, and wife Nella Yaacobi (from left to right).

With director Steven Spielberg, Jerry Stern (far left), and Rabbi Mark Schneier (far right) at the inauguration of the Hampton Synagogue in West Hampton, N.Y.

Trilateral meeting with Egypt's Ambassador to the United Nations, Dr. Nabil Elaraby (center), and PLO Observer to the United Nations, Dr. Nasser Al-Kidwa.

At home with Prime Minister Rabin and ambassadors from Arab countries. From left to right: Tunisia's Ambassador to the UN, Slaheddine Abdellah; Jordan's Ambassador, Adnan Abu Odeh; and Morocco's Ambassador, Ahmed Snoussi.

At home with Prime Minister Rabin and UN Secretary General Boutros Boutros-Ghali.

At home with Prime Minister Rabin and U.S. Ambassador to the UN, Dr. Madeleine Albright.

Establishing diplomatic relations with Namibia, 8 February 1994.

With Chairman of the Conference of Presidents of Major American Jewish Organization, (COP), Lester Pollack; (left), Executive Vice Chairman, Malcolm Hoenlein and Russian Ambassador to the United Nations, Yulif Vorontsov.

With Republican Senate Majority Leader Bob Dole.

Marching in New York's Salute to Israel Parade.

With Foreign Minister Shimon Peres and Security Council President for that month, Nigerian Ambassador to the UN, Prof. Ibrahim Gambari.

Addressing the United Nations General Assembly.

In the UN General Assembly with Foreign Minister Shimon Peres (front left) and Director General of the Ministry of Foreign Affairs, Uri Savir (front right).

Presenting my credentials to UN Secretary General Boutros Boutros-Ghali, October 1992.

Signing diplomatic relations with Ambassador Daudi Ngelautwa Mwakawago of Tanzania.

With Chairman of the Conference of Presidents of Major American Jewish Organizations (COP), Lester Pollack.

At the Special Session of the General Assembly Commemorating the Fiftieth Anniversary of the United Nations with Prime Minister Yitzhak Rabin and the other members of Israel's delegation. From left to right: Prime Minister Rabin; the Prime Minister's Advisor, Eitan Haber; Israel's Ambassador to the United States, Itamar Rabinovitch; former Foreign Minister Abba Eban.

Part Three
The Jewish People

6

A New Partnership: Israel and the Diaspora

The Pyramid of Personal Involvement

THE relationship between Israel and the Jewish people in Diaspora needs to be redefined. In that respect, the definition of Zionism also needs to be redefined since the definition offered by David Ben-Gurion many years ago was that a Zionist is no less than a person who makes aliyah to Israel.

In the years that have passed since then, it has become clear that this rather narrow definition has to be broadened enough to include Diaspora Jews who do not make aliyah but who do participate in the Israeli experience.

It is not only life in Israel and the continuity of the Zionist movement that we have to be concerned about, but also the continuity of Jewish life in America and the Diaspora's commitment to Israel.

Israelis do not have to struggle as much about their Jewish identity or the continuity of Jewish life as do Diaspora Jews. One does not have to be an observant Jew in Israel in order to experience Jewish life. Although the majority of Israelis are not religious, they live in Israel and are therefore part of the Jewish heritage. Their language is Hebrew, the language of the Jewish people; the schools they attend teach them the history of the Jewish people, the Bible, the Talmud, as part of a mandatory curriculum. Living in Israel guarantees that future generations will not be ignorant of the meaning of Judaism of the history and the heritage of the Jewish people, of a comprehensive Jewish identity. This is not the case for Diaspora Jews.

Not long ago, the relations between Israel and the Diaspora experienced a tense moment when the issue of "Who is a Jew" became the focus of political haggling. The demand of ultra-Orthodox politicians in Israel to redefine the meaning of who is a Jew and thus alienate American Reform and Conservative Jews was unacceptable to me at the time. It is also an argument that does not reflect the main problem, which to my mind is not, "Who is a Jew," but "Who will stay a Jew?" How many Diaspora Jews will still want to define themselves as Jewish in years to come? How can we ensure a continuation of Jewish life in the Diaspora?

The answer lies in three areas. The first is Jewish education. It is a question of whether the existing means to provide Jewish education in America are the answer when comprehensive Jewish education is not mandatory, not always affordable, and in most cases, is limited to religious contexts?

The second area is Jewish identity through religious life or through cultural affiliation with Jewish philosophy and Jewish ethics. Jewish life in America offers a variety of religious avenues of expression, mostly centered around synagogues of the different denominations. Unfortunately, one cannot find too many ways to be affiliated with Judaism through Jewish philosophy and Jewish ethics outside the synagogue.

The third area of Jewish identity is through relationships with the State of Israel and the people of Israel, which can be called Zionism. Defining Zionism only on the basis of aliyah does not reflect the situation in 1993, on the threshold of the twenty-first century.

The relations between Diaspora Jews and Israel in the early stages of the state were focused on the existential danger to Israel. At the end of the twentieth century, 4.2 million Jews live in Israel, and Israel to my mind does not face an existential danger anymore. I remember how David Ben-Gurion used to say, when he spoke about his vision of the State of Israel and the Jewish people, that once Israel reaches a population of five million Jews, it will then become safe from extinction. We are very close to achieving Ben-Gurion's vision today. Bringing Jews to Israel is still the main target and the message of Zionism, but we can deal with this today without the fear of annihilation.

The new Zionism has to be defined according to one's commitment to Israel and one's level of direct involvement with Israel. I call it the "Pyramid of Personal Involvement." The top of the pyramid is the one full commitment to life in Israel which is and always will be aliyah. But as we go down the pyramid, we can find other forms of personal commitment that may not be as complete but still can be defined as "Zionism." The second level just below aliyah is study and volunteer work in Israel. Third comes investments, tourism, and joint ventures—all three represent direct involvement in the Israeli economy. At the fourth level is formation of partnerships with Israeli firms, groups, universities, and research institutions. Level five consists of direct adoption of absorption centers, development towns, schools, and so on. At the sixth level are trips to Israel and participation in Israeli study groups, volunteer work for Israeli organizations, and the like. All those fall under the definition of Zionism. The lower levels of the pyramid describes non-Zionist activities.

Level seven takes us away from an active involvement in Israel to more passive support, such as Operation Exodus. Further down the pyramid, level eight is Jewish education and Jewish cultural life in the United States. Level nine comprises general support through UJA, Israel Bonds, and contributions to educational and cultural institutions in Israel. At the base of the pyramid is any kind of involvement in Jewish causes and Jewish life in the United States.

These different levels of personal commitment do not in any way try to place more value on one over another; they are all important and cherished. What it is meant to do is to scale a degree of commitment through Zionist activity and the relations between Diaspora Jews and Israel.

If we accept the Pyramid of Personal Involvement as the new agenda for Zionism, we have to create the vehicles to allow for the formation of new partnerships between Israelis and the Jewish people abroad. The American Zionist Movement should be the center to which other existing Zionist organizations, such as Hadassah, American Zionist Federation, Labor Zionists Alliance, Zionist Organization of America, National Committee of Labor Israel, Religious Zionists of America, and so forth, will gravitate. In addition to those existing organizations, new partnerships will be formed.

Those partnerships will be formed similar to the structure of what was known as Operation Independence. In Operation Independence, American businessmen and Israeli businessmen got together to explore joint ventures in Israel. The idea was to create opportunities for American businessmen, not only to make charitable contributions to support Israel or even to invest money in Israel, but also to get personally involved with their Israeli counterparts. This concept can be expanded to included other forms of partnerships. American physicians and Israeli physicians can work together on health issues in Israel, physicists and physicists, chemists and chemists, and the list can go on and on through all professions.

Other partnerships can be formed in the humanities, involving philosophers, historians, educators, and journalists. It can include the arts—theater, literature, and music. There could be other partnerships to deal with more complex endeavors, such as a partnership for tourism in Israel or a partnership for the advancement of high tech, infrastructure, or communications. The number of those partnerships can be as high as in the hundreds, and the number of participants can be in the thousands. The number of participants in each partnership can be as few as ten or twenty or as many as two hundred. And in each of them, American Jews and Israelis will work together on Israeli-related issues, creating direct dialogue and direct personal involvement. This will create a huge meeting place for American Jews and Israelis, and it will create a new process of personal commitment and personal involvement that we can call the new Zionism.

The Pyramid of Personal Involvement, helps show how American Jews can find a place for themselves in a new definition of Zionism. The American Zionist Movement should create those new partnerships in which Americans and Israelis will work together. Other than making aliyah, it is only through personal commitment and direct involvement that an American Jew can be a Zionist.

Based on a keynote address before the American Zionist Movement, 24 March 1993. Article published in *The North American Jewish Forum Magazine*, winter 1993/1994.

Reflections on the Pyramid of Personal Involvement

In my address to the American Zionist Movement in March 1993, I presented a redefinition of Zionism according to the individual's commitment to Israel and level of direct involvement with Israel. The new definition was based on the Pyramid of Personal Involvement, and necessarily, in general order of priority.

The pyramid describes how *people,* not institutions, express their commitment to Israel, and it measures this commitment by levels of *direct* involvement. At the top of the pyramid, of course, is full commitment to life in Israel—aliyah.

Different individuals will have different levels of involvement with Israel and its institutions such as Hadassah Hospital, the Jewish National Fund, and the like. In no way does the pyramid assign relative value to the work these organizations do. What the pyramid does tell us is that among people who affiliate with such organizations, those whose involvement is more active and direct have reached higher levels of Zionist actualization than those whose involvement is more passive and indirect.

The pyramid's levels are divided into two main groups: Zionist and non-Zionist. Zionist activities are distinguished by activity in Israel itself: aliyah, study programs, investment, partnerships, adoption of communities, and so forth. Non-Zionist activities are characterized either by indirect involvement with Israel, such as passive support through philanthropic donations, or by focusing activity in the Diaspora.

Political activism on Israel's behalf, including *hasbarah* activities, promote Israel to non-Israeli publics. Because it does not focus on work in Israel itself, this activity is not defined as Zionist. Rather it is considered pro-Israel work, and its importance is of the first order. Here, it is appropriate to emphasize once again, that the pyramid does not try to place more value on one type of activity over another. Rather, it is designed to measure an individual's direct involvement with Israel.

The Israel-Diaspora partnership and Jewish continuity can be strengthened by effective Jewish education.

By its very nature, Jewish education includes Zionist education and the study of Hebrew. At the root of all Jewish culture stands the Hebrew language. The Bible, our literature, our philosophy and poetry—expressions of the Jewish spirit—are intimately bound up in the Hebrew tongue. Other vernaculars have come and gone, but Hebrew remains the thread uniting them all. This is our heritage, and it cannot be fully appreciated or internalized in translation.

Not only is the Hebrew language a connection with the past. It is also a connection with the present and the future. In several decades, the majority of the world's Jewish population will live in Israel. To engage in a serious dialogue with Israelis, Diaspora Jewry must understand the Hebrew language and culture it is producing.

Direct involvement in Israel is critical to the Israel-Diaspora relationship. A redefinition of Zionism that accounts for the levels of personal involvement can contribute to a richer, more creative partnership between our communities.

Written in June 1994.

The Jews and Israel: Myth and Reality

A number of articles have recently appeared in *Ha'aretz* and other Israeli newspapers regarding seeming alienation, hostility, and deep division between American Jews and Israel. Several of the assessments focus on a so-called distancing between the respective positions of the Israeli government and the organized Jewish community in the United States.

It seems to me that these descriptions—often by those who wish to be seen as "patriots" of the Labor Party—are not based on personal knowledge of the reality in America, and do not accurately reflect the situation. At the very least they do not accurately reflect what I have witnessed over the course of many meetings throughout the United States during the past year.

I do not believe that one can make a definitive, sweeping declaration about the state of relations between Israel and the Diaspora or between the American Jewish establishment and the Israeli government. We are speaking of a vast continent, with many active communities, about 5.5 million Jews, and tens of thousands of lay and professional leaders in the Federations, local Jewish organizations, and national organizations.

During the past year I have participated in over one hundred public gatherings with Jews from major American cities such as New York, Los Angeles, Chicago, Boston, Detroit, Miami, Atlanta, Columbus, Memphis, and others. I have seen among American Jewry and among the Jewish establishment a diversity of opinion spanning the range of viewpoints the we express in Israel.

There is a tendency, however, to adopt the policy and positions of whatever government happens to be serving in Israel at the time. The notable exception is found among groups and individuals whose position regarding the territories tends toward annexation or compromise. It is reasonable to assume that the rest feel that because they do not live in Israel and do not vote for the Knesset or government, they have an obligation to support the policies of the democratically elected government of Israel and to assist in their achievement. This was recently expressed in the changes in AIPAC and in statements by heads of the Anti-Defamation League, the Conference of Presidents, the American Jewish Congress, and the American Jewish Committee.

I believe that the central problem is not the extent of American Jewish support for the Israeli government, but the extent of their activity to preserve a vital Jewish community in the United States and to develop the partnership with Israel.

Unfortunately, the number of Jews involved in communal activities is on the decline. The reasons are well known: assimilation, growing distance from the generation of immigrants, inadequate

Jewish education, and so forth. For them, the main question is no longer, "Who is a Jew?" but rather, "Who will stay a Jew?"

A normative-cultural gap exists between Israelis and American Jews. They and we live in different cultures, speak different languages, and have different experiences. Our responses to similar phenomena will therefore also be different.

The key to improving the situation lies in strengthening the partnership between us. This includes the establishment of new frameworks for exposing more Israelis to American visitors and vice versa; for economic cooperation—investment, exports, and tourism; for cooperation and exchange of knowledge in science, technology, health, and culture; for dialogue on issues of Jewish identity and meaning; and for exploring further ways to expand the partnership between us.

As direct and personal connections between Israel and the Diaspora grow, mutual understanding will increase, and the feelings of alienation will be left behind.

Based on a Hebrew article originally published in *Ha'aretz*, 23 August 1993.

Israel and Diaspora: Creating a New Partnership

As Israel and the Arabs take bold steps toward peace, the historic changes sweeping the Middle East challenge Diaspora Jews, especially in the United States, to redefine their relationship with Israel.

The vast majority of Jews in America supports Israel's agreements with the PLO. A recent poll shows that approximately 90 percent approve of the mutual recognition agreement and 74 percent support the Declaration of Principles. Although these numbers come as no surprise, they contradict earlier estimates that attempted to raise fears among the Israeli leadership regarding the extent of support it could expect from American Jewry in particular and Diaspora Jewry in general.

For decades, the organized American Jewish community has affirmed a responsibility to support the policy of any democratically elected government in Israel. Sharp changes in policy through the years have subsequently generated similarly dramatic shifts in the opinions expressed by Jewish organizations. Indeed, American Jewry seems to have flip-flopped on certain issues to such an extent that Michael Kinsley sarcastically asked in *The New Republic*

(11 October 1993), "[Shouldn't] you be a bit suspicious of your own opinions if they change 180 degrees overnight?"

But in contrast to this adaptability regarding specific policy issues, American Jewry, throughout the years, has rigidly held to one fundamental view of Israel-Diaspora relations. Diaspora Jews have traditionally based their identification with Israel on the need to provide material and moral support to an embattled country whose very existence was in danger. At times, they have also relied on the need for practical assistance to aid the absorption of Jewish immigrants fleeing persecution in countries such as Ethiopia and the former Soviet Union. But now, the recent progress toward peace and coexistence and the thaw in Israel's relations with several Muslim countries have struck at the underpinnings of this old formulation of the Israel-Diaspora relationship.

Despite overwhelming support for the agreements, American Jews seem concerned about the basis of their relationship with Israel. The agreements and their aftermath have made clear what has already been the case for some time. Israel is not a poor cousin that needs charity and protection to survive.

The elimination of the existential threat as a central theme creates a vacuum in American Jewish identity that the transition to "positive messages" cannot fill overnight. The relationship between the Jews and Israel will, accordingly, undergo substantial change.

In the meantime, there is much uncertainty about the satisfaction with these new developments and the change they will engender. American Jewry now faces the difficult task of forming completely new frameworks, directions, and understandings. These are slow and significant processes. Eventually, the revolution in consciousness will create a different Diaspora identity and a new partnership with Israel.

We must see a shift in emphasis, away from charity and donations and towards investment and joint ventures in industry, research, science, tourism, and education.

True partnership, however, implies a reciprocal relationship. In the wake of rampant assimilation and intermarriage, American Jews should be placing an even greater emphasis on Jewish continuity, education, and culture in the Diaspora itself. In this effort, Israel can and should play a role.

By now, it is well known in the Jewish community that spending time in Israel increases commitment and activism. The nineteenth-century philosopher Ahad Ha'am had a vision of a Jewish state that would serve as the spiritual center of the Jewish people. By encouraging a direct connection with Israel and Israelis, and by helping to strengthen Jewish communities around the world, Israel can truly fulfill that role.

More and more Diaspora Jews are beginning to understand that, despite the threats that still exist, Israel no longer confronts the existential question, "To be or not to be?" Rather, today's defining questions address the quality of life. How can Israel maximize its human potential to construct a better social and economic future?

American Jews understand that this question will be answered primarily by the Israelis. Given this fact, they ask, what will be their new role in the Israel-Diaspora relationship?

The two communities must work together to answer this question and, thus, determine the future nature and quality of relations between them. In its broadest outlines, the answer we provide must construct a true partnership in the building of Israel's economy and society. It must strengthen Jewish identity and knowledge in the Diaspora. And above all, it must establish a continuing and open dialogue between Israelis and American Jews so that our partnership will thrive.

Article originally published in *The Jerusalem Post*, 9 November 1993.

The Role of Israel in Jewish Education

As a crisis of continuity grips Diaspora Jewry, the question, "Who is a Jew?" has been replaced by the more urgent, "Who will stay a Jew?" More and more Diaspora Jews are realizing that Israel and Jewish education are two major components of the answer.

Israel's role in Diaspora Jewish education reflects the Israel-Diaspora relationship as a whole. Through education, which includes personal example and general leadership, adults perpetuate values and norms and teach children what is important to the community. The newfound emphasis on Israel in Jewish education is only one part of a multifaceted attempt to create a new Israel-Diaspora partnership.

The new situation in Israel and the Diaspora demand the creation of a new partnership between the communities. Direct involvement with Israel is crucial for Jewish identity in Diaspora and for social and economic development in Israel. This means spending time in Israel, developing professional partnerships, social relationships, and direct investment in the economy.

Our new partnership will have to extend to education. Israel has benefited greatly from contact with Diaspora Jewish professors and students. Likewise, Israel can offer much to teachers and students in the Diaspora to strengthen the education necessary for Jewish continuity.

Israel's role in the Jewish school should be aimed at achieving four main goals:

1. Teach every teacher and student Hebrew.

2. Provide educational experiences in Israel for as many students as possible.

3. Encourage partnerships among Israeli and Diaspora teachers.

4. Provide models for curricula in Jewish culture.

Hebrew

At the root of all Jewish culture stands the Hebrew language. The Bible, our literature, philosophy, poetry—expressions of the Jewish spirit—are intimately bound up in the Hebrew tongue. Other vernaculars have come and gone, but Hebrew has remained the thread uniting them all. This is our heritage, and it cannot be fully appreciated or internalized in translation.

The Hebrew language is also a connection with the 4.5 million Jews living in Israel. To engage in a serious dialogue with Israelis, Diaspora Jewry must understand the Hebrew language and culture that shape them.

Knowledge of Hebrew should be required of all teachers in Jewish schools. Israel, in partnership with Diaspora schools, can expand Hebrew training for teachers. It can also provide native Hebrew speakers to teach the language in Jewish schools. Already, a significant number of Israelis fill this role.

Teaching children Hebrew will strengthen their connection to Jewish culture and the Jewish people. But more than this, it will strengthen the Jewish community as a whole. Parents who take an interest in their children's education often learn along with their children. The establishment in 1898 of the first Hebrew kindergartens in Eretz Yisrael helped many parents learn Hebrew from their children and led to the rebirth of Hebrew as a living language.

To succeed, innovative and more intensive education may be required. Working together, Israelis and Diaspora Jews can examine options for such programs as Hebrew kindergartens and day care centers, adult education programs, and other methods of promoting Hebrew literacy among Diaspora Jews.

Study in Israel

The most effective way to learn a language, of course, is to live where it is spoken. Thousands of Diaspora Jews have participated in ulpanim and other educational programs in Israel. Semester and year programs give high school and college students broad educational experiences that extend far beyond the classroom walls.

These programs not only provide intensive Jewish, Hebrew, and Israeli studies, but also give Diaspora Jews a direct connection to Israel and Israelis. In Israel, these young Jews are exposed at a formative stage in their lives to a vibrant Jewish culture that encompasses all areas of life.

Shorter summer programs in Israel also provide good extracurricular education. For those who cannot spend more than a few weeks in Israel, these programs are all the more important. Of course, there is no reason why young Jews should not participate in both. Education should not be limited to formal schooling. Jewish schools would be wise to explore ways to encourage students to participate in all these programs, recognizing that the more time a student spends in Israel, the more he or she will benefit from the experience. We should aspire to bring as many young Jews as possible to be educated in Israel.

Teacher Partnerships

The best teachers are those who lead by example. As role models for their students, teachers should exemplify the Israel-Diaspora partnership. By exchanging ideas and knowledge, engaging in joint research, twinning classrooms, and working together on a host of other projects, Israeli and Diaspora Jewish teachers can widen the horizons for Jewish education in both places.

Such partnerships can focus on areas of concern to both parties, Israeli-related issues, education-related issues, and Diaspora-related issues. The partnerships will be similar in structure to what was known as Operation Independence. In Operation Independence, American and Israeli businessmen embarked on joint ventures in Israel. The idea was to create opportunities for American businessmen, not only to make charitable contributions to support

Israel or even to invest money in Israel, but also to get personally involved with their Israeli counterparts.

Israel and the Diaspora have much to learn from each other. Teacher partnerships will create a direct dialogue and direct personal involvement, creating a new meeting place for Israelis and Diaspora Jews to strengthen their relationship.

Curriculum Models

Israel's public school system has been committed to providing Jewish children with Jewish knowledge and values since its establishment. It has designed curricula to achieve this goal and has invested much energy and resources in developing quality Jewish education.

Israel is eager to share its know-how and experience in this area with Diaspora Jewry. But we recognize that every community has conditions unique to it. Jewish education in a Jewish state will necessarily differ from Jewish education in Diaspora. For Israel's Jewish population, Jewish education is mandatory, free, and comprehensive. In America and other communities, such education is voluntary, often expensive, and generally limited to religious contexts.

There is room for change. Affordable Jewish education that incorporates religious and secular aspects of Jewish life can be established if a concerted effort is made. Israeli curricula can be adopted and adapted to suit local needs in Diaspora Jewish schools.

****

Holding Jewish education as one of its supreme values, the Zionist movement early on sought to establish a national university in Jerusalem. At the dedication of the Hebrew University on 24 July 1918, Chaim Weizmann declared, "In this university we have gone beyond restoration; we are creating . . . something which is to serve as the symbol of a better future."

We too can set our sights higher than merely preserving what exists. If we look beyond preserving continuity, we can aspire to a renaissance of Jewish life. Working together, Israel and Diaspora can develop Jewish education and a kind of partnership that will strengthen Jews' ties to their heritage and to each other, no matter where they live.

Article originally published in *Jewish Education Magazine,* fall 1994.

7

Israel: Building a Nation

Immigration and Integration in the Land of Israel

A tiny country, just reaching its forty-fifth birthday, Israel has assumed its rightful place among the nations. The birth of our nation and its subsequent development haven't been easy. "If only Moses had taken a left turn and not a right," we joke, referring to our lack of natural resources. We have no oil; we have little water. In fact, much of the land is a desert. Nonetheless, we are rich in the most important resource of all—our people.

And our people have come, and continue to come, from all over the world. We began as a nation of immigrants. The creation of the State of Israel is rooted in the Jewish people's fervent hope to return to their ancestral homeland, from which we were exiled two thousand years ago. It rests on the idea of "the ingathering of the exiles" or as we say in Hebrew, *aliyah*. In other words, immigration is the raison d'etre of the State of Israel—the land of our birth; the land of our history, where our first thousand years are recorded in the Bible; the land where our cultural, religious, and national identity was forged; the land where we have kept an unbroken presence through the millennia. In 1948, the State of Israel was formed, and the world recognized what we have known forever. We were now formally able to come home. And we did. In droves.

Of course, immigration occurred a long time before the establishment of the State of Israel.

We all know that throughout history, the Jewish people have been repeatedly dispersed by its enemies. In spite of this, we never abandoned the constant desire to return to the land of our forefathers. This unprecedented sociocultural phenomenon helped us keep our language and traditions alive. From the time of the expulsion and destruction of the Temple in Jerusalem in 70 C.E., we have kept Jerusalem, the center of Jewish spiritual life since biblical times, in our daily prayers, believing we would someday return. Our strong communal and religious institutions, and a deep and abiding faith, fueled this hope. We experienced periods of prosperity and growth as well as hardship and persecution, all the while trying to maintain a presence in the Land of Israel.

In the late nineteenth century, with the continued oppression and persecution of Jews in Eastern Europe and anti-Semitism rampant all over the continent, the longing for Jerusalem and the Land of Israel, or "Zion," found formal expression. This was the movement of Zionism outlined at the first World Zionist Congress, convened by Theodore Herzl in Switzerland. Aimed at attaining an internationally recognized and secure home in the Land of Zion, where Jews could live in peace and harmony without fear of discrimination, young pioneers came to Palestine. They came to help nourish this precious piece of earth, to drain swamps, and to make bare hillsides bloom. But, above all, they came to build a new life for themselves. To this day, Jews all over the world refer to Israel as *Haaretz,* the Hebrew word for "the land." You will still find Jews arriving in Israel for the first time bending down to kiss the earth.

After its conquest of the area in World War I, Great Britain issued the Balfour Declaration on 2 November 1917, committing itself to establishing a Jewish national home in Palestine. During the British Mandate (from 1922 to 1948) granted by the League of Nations, there were waves of immigration and the country developed rapidly. Towns and villages were built, social and health service systems were established, and educational networks were put in place.

As the Nazis gained power in Germany in the early 1930s and the Jews experienced harsher and harsher measures of discrimination and persecution, several different rescue operations aimed at bringing Jews home to the Promised Land were organized. The Youth Aliyah operation is among the most well known—it brought more than five thousand Jewish teenagers to Palestine, educating them in boarding schools throughout the country.

In 1939, in response to Arab pressure, the British placed severe restrictions on the number of Jews allowed to immigrate to Palestine. This was called the MacDonald White Paper. While the situation of Jews in Europe was quickly deteriorating, other countries of the world refused to make allowances in their strict immigrant quotas. Chaim Weizmann, who was later to become Israel's first president, summarized the situation. For the Jews, the world was divided into "places where they cannot enter" and "places where they cannot live."

Following World War II, Holocaust survivors were still not allowed to enter Palestine. Hoping to save their brethren, those Jews already living there organized an illegal immigration network. "Aliyah Bet," as this network was called, brought more than eighty-five thousand refugees to the homeland, on old broken and battered boats that miraculously managed to get through the British blockade.

And then, after the world witnessed the genocidal destruction of six million Jews in the Nazi Holocaust of World War II, the necessity of a Jewish homeland was no longer just a Jewish dream.

The State of Israel was proclaimed on 14 May 1948; the Declaration of the Establishment of the State of Israel not only outlines the framework of the democratic Jewish State, but also recognizes its historical roots and its existence as the homeland for the Jewish people. I quote:

In the Land of Israel the Jewish people came into being. In this Land was shaped their spiritual, religious, and national character. Here they lived in sovereign independence. Here they created a culture of national and universal import, and gave to the world the eternal Book of Books.

Exiled by force, still the Jewish people kept faith with their Land in all the countries of their dispersion, steadfast in their prayer and hope to return and here revive their political freedom.

Fired by this attachment of history and tradition, the Jews in every generation strove to renew their roots in the ancient homeland, and in recent generations they came home in their multitudes. . . .

The Holocaust that in our time destroyed millions of Jews in Europe and again proved beyond doubt the compelling need to solve the problem of Jewish homelessness and dependence by the renewal of the Jewish State in the Land of Israel, which would open wide the gates of the homeland to every Jew and endow the Jewish people with the status of a nation with equality of rights within the family of nations. . . .

The State of Israel shall be open to Jewish immigration and the ingathering of exiles. It will devote itself to developing the Land for the good of all its inhabitants. . . .

We call upon the Jewish people throughout the Diaspora to join forces with us in immigration and construction, and to be at our right hand in the great endeavor to fulfil the age-old longing for the redemption of Israel.

The Law of Return, passed in 1950, reiterates this idea, granting every Jew the right to return to Israel and, upon entry, to automatically acquire citizenship. It gives legal confirmation to the age-old yearning for the return to Zion as spelled out at the First Zionist Congress in 1897 to Jewish immigration to the land as stated in Article 6 of the Mandate for Palestine granted Great Britain by the League of Nations in 1922, and to the concept of "the ingathering of the exiles," which lies at the heart of the Declaration of the Establishment of the State of Israel.

After the establishment of the State, Israel became an active participant in several emergency rescue operations, the latest one being "Operation Solomon," which brought fifteen thousand immigrants to Israel from Ethiopia on forty direct flights over less than two days. The Israel Defense Forces used their own planes together with El Al aircraft to evacuate the thousand of people who fled the countryside to seek refuge at Israel's Embassy in Addis Ababa. Organizing the crowds, providing food and medical supplies, and coordinating complicated arrangements under intense pressure added to the complexity of the operation.

Huge cargo planes were used, without seats, to maximize the amount of passengers. There was no luggage. The few belongings that some of the passengers had were tied to their backs. The tired, frightened, yet grateful Ethiopian Jews sat, cross-legged, in complete silence, in row after row of mattresses that covered the floor of the plane.

With "Operation Moses" in 1984, conducted in secrecy amid great internal strife within Ethiopia itself, still another seven thousand Ethiopian Jews were brought to Israel, after having fled to Sudan from where they were then rescued in a massive airlift. Because Operation Moses was aborted before its completion due to reports in the news media, the Israeli government was determined to bring all those Ethiopian Jews desiring to return home to Israel. Today, fewer than two thousand Ethiopian Jews remain in Ethiopia, and Israel is committed to bringing them home.

Other rescue operations include:

- "Operation Magic Carpet," the code name for Israel's rescue from Yemen, which brought us forty-five thousand people between 1948 and 1950.
- "Operation Ezra and Nehemiah," the rescue mission from Iraq, brought us more than 110,000 Jews between 1948 and 1950. These new immigrants came in two thousand direct flights from Baghdad or via Cyprus.
- About twenty-five thousand Jews were brought to Israel from

Iran between 1949 and 1950. On the eve of Khomeini's rise to power, another two thousand were brought home.

- About thirty-two thousand Jews were brought to Israel from Libya between 1949 and 1951.
- Between 1959 and 1965, the Mossad carried out "Operation Yachin," in which 250,000 Jews from Morocco were brought to Israel to join their fellow North Africans (from Tunisia and Algeria) who had been brought to Israel intermittently since the creation of the State.
- More than three hundred thousand Jews have come to Israel from Romania since 1948.

The list goes on and on.

Since the birth of the State, Israel has absorbed more than two million immigrants. In the first four years alone, Israel's population doubled, and during the last four years, more than one-half million have come. This is a huge number, especially for a tiny state such as ours. It is like having thirty-five million immigrants coming to the United States from non-English-speaking countries—people without private capital, without formal democratic backgrounds; people unfamiliar with your way of life and the norms of your culture.

Yet there is a dramatic difference between this hypothetical immigration to the United States and our recent waves of immigration to Israel. Although the Soviet Jews and Ethiopian Jews were coming to a country with which they were unfamiliar, they were still coming home. And seeing their tears of joy as they kissed the land when they disembarked from our El Al jets was an experience I shall never forget.

The aliya from the Soviet Union was the realization of a dream not only for those coming to Israel, but also for those of us already there, who had been struggling for years, clandestinely and openly, for their release. You are all familiar with the stories of anguish, the separation of families, the long, frustrating waits that our Soviet brethren had to endure. And then the gates were opened.

We welcomed hordes of highly professional immigrants. As they came off the planes, one after the other was carrying a violin. When a newcomer came down the steps without a musical instrument, we knew that he or she was the pianist.

Today, when you ask a Russian, "How was your life in the Soviet Union?" he answers, "I could not complain." "And how do you feel in Israel?" He answers, "Now I can complain." And he *does* complain—showing that he is certainly becoming an Israeli.

The potential of Israel's new immigrants is enormous. We are absorbing doctors and scientists, scholars and musicians, technicians and teachers. We are also absorbing farmers and peasants, unskilled workers and rural villagers—people unfamiliar with modern technology and sophisticated methodologies; people with personal goals and dreams, emotions ranging from deep gratitude to impatience and fear and regret; people with preconceived ideas and commitments to past and future hopes. But one thing remains strong amid the happiness, confusion, and despair—and that is faith. Faith in their dream and faith in ours.

Massive immigration causes waves of change in any country, often fostering resentment and even hatred—as we are witnessing in Europe today. In Israel we too face difficulties, hardship, and sacrifice whenever there is a huge influx of newcomers. However, unlike other countries of the world, Israel has not only always welcomed new immigrants—we have sought them out.

We have a tremendous task ahead of us. In real terms absorbing these newcomers will cost us twenty-four billion dollars. We must invest in new housing, new infrastructure (roads, parks, expansion of existing facilities), new schools, training and retraining programs, education and language study, as well as manpower in the form of teachers, social workers, family therapists, and administrators.

You can see that this is an enormous challenge. It takes from four to six years to "absorb" a new immigrant, to make him feel that he is no longer a new immigrant, but an Israeli. The initial phase places great stress on the Israeli society as a whole and certainly on the newcomer.

I myself was born in Palestine—to parents who were themselves new immigrants. They came to Palestine separately—my father from Byelorussia in 1923 and my mother about four years later from the Ukraine. They came with other youngsters but without their families. They came because of their strong idealism, to a place they did not know, a place they had only heard about, joining another 150,000 people (the same number of immigrants that came to Israel last year alone) to help build up the Jewish homeland. Not particularly religious, they came as Jewish pioneers. Rather courageous, I must say, when I think about it now. And they came with the blessings of their parents. Also, rather courageous, demonstrating the strength of my grandparents' dreams for their children. My mother's parents were wise enough to follow their daughter—they came in 1937. Unfortunately, my father's parents remained behind; they and the rest of his whole family were exterminated.

Together with other members of their group, my parents first established a kibbutz in the Jezreel Valley, Gvat. Later, in 1930, a core group established a cooperative village—Kfar Vitkin. For those of you who know Israel, Kfar Vitkin is along the coast between Netanya and Hadera. For those of you not so familiar with my country's geography, it's between Tel Aviv and Haifa, on the seashore. After three to four years, we received new immigrants from Germany and Turkey, and then, after World War II, illegal refugees escaping from Europe and the British Mandate authorities found shelter on our *moshav*—the Hebrew word for cooperative settlement.

When I served in the new Israeli army, I served with new immigrants from Morocco. And directly after the army, I was involved in youth instruction, helping to build new moshavim—in the Negev, the Galilee, and the Lachish area. In fact, during a seven-year period, (from 1950 to 1957), four hundred new moshavim were established in Israel. Until 1950, only seventy had been established from the time the first moshav—Nahalal—was founded in the 1920s. In ten years time, the new moshavim became a major component in Israeli life, politically and in the agricultural sector. Many Knesset members, army generals, and cabinet ministers, including Moshe Dayan, Ariel Sharon, and Rafael Eitan, grew up on moshavim. Many others are kibbutzim members, including the former Prime Minister Levi Eshkol, the former Chief of Staff Dan Shomron, and the present Chief of Staff Ehud Barak.

All our prime ministers—besides Yitzhak Rabin—can be called ex-immigrants—David Ben-Gurion, Moshe Sharett, Levi Eshkol, and Golda Meir, who was born in Kiev and grew up in the States. Both Shimon Peres and Yitzhak Shamir came from Poland. Also, all of Israel's presidents, besides Yitzhak Navon, were at one time new immigrants. However, as the country has grown, the number of our native Israelis is rapidly growing. In fact, the majority of Israel's Knesset members are already native Israelis.

Of its nearly five million people, about 82 percent are Jews. Today, more than half those Jews are native-born, mostly first and second generation, from places as far away in geography and culture as Yemen and Eastern Europe, the former Soviet Union, and Ethiopia. Of the remaining 18 percent, about 16 percent are Arabs, mostly Muslim. Both our country and our society are rather young—the median age today is twenty-five and a half years. Lifestyles range from contemporary to traditional, from urban to rural, from secular to orthodox, from collective to individual.

The population of Israel has grown six fold since statehood was declared. We were 650,000 in 1947; today we number 4,400,000. Of course, this enormous growth has a major impact on all levels.

Economically, the GNP, in real terms, is thirty-five times greater than what it was in 1947. Culturally and artistically, Israel has also grown tremendously. Our first musicians were immigrants. The painters Reuven Rubin, Avigdor Stematsky, and Mordechai Ardon came from Europe. Israel's national theater, "Habimah" (meaning "the stage"), was established in Tel Aviv in 1931, brought from Moscow under the guidance of the Russian director Constantin Stanislavsky and the actress Hanna Rovina, who later became the "First Lady of Hebrew Theater." Many of our most beloved poets were also immigrants—Haim Nahman Bialik (1873–1934) and Saul Tchernichovsky (1875–1943).

Hebrew prose in the Land of Israel was first written by immigrant writers whose literature was often a mixture of their roots and traditions and the challenge and promise of building up the homeland. Yosef Haim Brenner (1881–1921) and Shmuel Yosef Agnon (1888–1970), who both came from Europe, are considered by many as the fathers of modern Hebrew literature. In 1966, Agnon received the Nobel prize for literature.

Besides changing the nature of Israel's economic and cultural life, immigration has also opened up Israel in the international arena. Creating a new versatility in Israel itself, new immigrants taught us to think internationally, enabling us to forge links and build bridges with the other nations of the world. Israel is today part of the European Economic Community (EEC); we also have a special agreement with the United States in the free trade area. And although 70 percent of the Jewish people are still living abroad—that is, outside of Israel—their participation in our lives is an integral part of our growth—both unprecedented and invaluable.

Born of idealism and a dream, built through hard work and struggle—at the conference table, on the land, at the university, and on the battlefield—Israel is home to a widely diverse population, coming from more than one hundred countries throughout the world.

A modern country with ancient roots, Israel is composed of a vastly rich mosaic of people, a place where East meets West, where the past meets the present, and where people of totally different backgrounds come together to form a strong, heterogeneous population. Once a society of immigrants, Israel's present cultural life is like a cloth woven together with many different fibers.

A state less than fifty years old, with a heritage more than four thousand years old, a modern Western democratic nation in a Middle Eastern context, surrounded by nondemocratic Muslim countries, Israel is struggling to create an identity uniquely its own, while still preserving the history and culture of its varied communities.

In the search for an Israeli identity, this diversity fosters a dynamic creative tension in a country where change is swift and sharp. Each period produces new challenges and struggles as well as new artists and movements in an atmosphere of constant growth and stimulation. This is at once tiring and exhilarating, a dichotomy of old and new, variety and unity, adding to the vibrancy of our very old, very young nation.

The absorption or integration of new immigrants into any existing society is a major challenge for which I can proudly say that Israel's experience can serve as a model or pilot project. Motivated by our cultural heritage, national identity, and Zionist idealism, we are the only people in the world that have developed an "absorption" infrastructure. We have pioneered the "ulpan" language-teaching program that has proven that intensive language training is the most successful.

With the large numbers of Soviet and Ethiopian immigrants that have recently been welcomed home, we have greatly enriched the fabric of our society. Our brainpower is our major advantage—our universities and research and development centers stand among the best in the world.

Now is the time to harness that brainpower, to direct our efforts toward growth and development in our region, together with our Arab neighbors. We are hopeful the peace process will move forward, so we can all live in security and prosperity, and together build a future where our children and grandchildren can devote themselves to human development. Peace is the only foundation upon which we can achieve our full potential.

A peaceful environment could free up thirty billion annually from defense costs and channel it to progress and development. Moreover, it would also gradually allow:

- The establishment of a Middle Eastern Common Market;
- The creation of joint ventures based on integrated knowledge and capital together with mineral resources from both inside and outside the region;
- The establishment of an integrated network of infrastructure for ports, airports, and railways (for example, a train from

Cairo to Damascus, a seaport in Gaza serving Jordan, a Jordanian-Israeli airport in Akaba-Eilat on the Red Sea, and a joint electrical energy and desalination plant in Sinai;

- The opening of borders for tourism;
- The cooperation in the fields of health, professional training, technology, and agriculture.

Political unreadiness and short sightedness have littered the history of the Middle East with wasted opportunities for a breakthrough to peace, at a tragic price. It is my hope that the lesson has been learned and great opportunities will bring about great and courageous decisions.

Only when the guns fall silent and the peoples of the region can devote themselves to improving their quality of life rather than to military confrontation and futile hatred, will the Middle East once again become a model civilization. At stake are the lives and well-being of hundreds of millions of people and the future of us all.

Clearly, we have major issues to grapple with, none simple, none easy, but with our past experience and new citizens we stand stronger, more whole, ready to face the tasks ahead of us.

Excerpted from a speech delivered at Memphis State University on 28 February 1993.

Remarks upon Receiving the Golda Meir Human Relations Award

I am honored to accept the Golda Meir Human Relations Award of NA'AMAT-USA. I knew Golda personally for many years. Thus, I am especially moved that you selected me to be the recipient of this award.

It is also a privilege for me to be recognized by NA'AMAT, which has done so much to improve the lives and well-being of the people of Israel. I have long been involved and impressed with the work you are doing in a range of areas. After all, my mother was a member of NA'AMAT, and my wife is still a member. So, I am, in a sense, a son and a spouse of NA'AMAT. I thank you again for this honor.

It is hard to believe that it has been fifteen years since Golda passed away. She was a remarkable and forceful personality.

Her life exemplified service to the greater good and the common cause of the Jewish people and the State of Israel. Indeed, her life embodied the modern saga of Zionism. She was born in Kiev, at a time when oppression and the fear of pogroms cast a shadow over Eastern European Jewry. Her family fled to the United States and settled in Milwaukee.

Like countless others, Golda could easily have tried to put the past behind her, to forget about the suffering and persecution that the Jews endured. But that was not her way. Golda became active in the Zionist movement and left the comfort and freedom of America for the trials of Palestine. She was a pioneer and idealist. As I was born in Palestine, in the Land of Israel, to parents who made aliyah in 1923, and I did not have the privilege of experiencing this personal endeavor, I admire those people for their courage and devotion.

She served her people with distinction and became one of the most popular and well-known public figures in the world. She was known, simply, affectionately, as Golda. It was a testament to the affection that the people felt for her.

I remember one of our personal talks about a very crucial state matter: the need to make progress toward an interim settlement with Egypt in 1971. We had some differences of opinion on this matter. As I was a young member of the Knesset at the time, I felt uneasy about arguing with her because she was the prime minister. So she told me, "Don't feel uneasy because you are young. If you believe you are right then be honest and stick to it. After all," Golda told me, "being young is a defect which passes very soon, based on my own experience," and she was right, unfortunately.

Throughout Jewish history, women have played a leading role in shaping our people. Golda was very much a product of that tradition. Like Queen Esther, she stood up to the enemies of Israel. Like Deborah the judge, she ruled with devotion. And like Sarah, Rivka, Rachel, and Leah, she devoted her life to building a nation.

That Golda succeeded in reaching the heights of political power is eloquent testimony to the advanced nature of Israeli society.

Golda was the only American Jew to sign the Israeli Declaration of Independence, and she rose to the highest leadership posts. If Golda were alive today, she would be proud to see how Israel has opened its arms and its hearts to welcome the thousands of new immigrants arriving every month.

We are proud that the Jewish population of Israel has grown sevenfold since 1948, mainly due to aliyah. In the past few years, half a million new immigrants have arrived, primarily from the former Soviet Union and Ethiopia. It is as if 30 million new immigrants were to arrive in the United States who do not speak English and who come from nondemocratic backgrounds. It is our duty. It is our raison d'etre.

We saw so much war and so much bloodshed. Yet this only strengthened our conviction about the need for peace. In an address at the United Nations on 1 March 1957, Golda said, "Can we, from now on, all of us, turn over a new leaf and instead of fighting with each other, can we all, united, fight poverty and disease and illiteracy? . . . There is no limit to what we are prepared to contribute so that all of us together can live to see a day of happiness. . . ." Israelis and Arabs are now talking directly to achieve peace and a better future.

One of the most difficult moments of our lives came in the aftermath of the Yom Kippur War, which was a tragedy for the people and for Golda, in May 1974. Three armed Palestinian terrorists infiltrated from Lebanon and burst into the town of Maalot. They captured four teachers and ninety schoolchildren and threatened to kill them all unless Israel set free dozens of imprisoned terrorists. At the same time, the American mediator for the separation of forces agreement, Henry Kissinger, was in Israel. The Israeli army stormed the building where the terrorists were holed up and killed all three of them. In the exchange of fire, however, twenty teenagers were killed.

The next day, the Israeli cabinet faced the question of whether to give up on the Syrian-Israeli negotiations. Kissinger was deeply impressed when Golda told him that Israel would proceed with the negotiations. Her logic was clear: war and terrorism are a symptom of the fundamental disease of a lack of peace. Negotiations are the only remedy. "We had all better get back to peacemaking," she said. It was truly one of Golda's noblest moments. And it is in that spirit that we must face the challenges that lie ahead.

Israel continues to strive to fulfill the vision of a Middle East free of conflict and suffering. We want to replace the tragedy of war with the fruits of peace. We want to leave behind the pain of the past and focus instead on the promise of a better tomorrow. We now have a historic opportunity to change the face of the Middle East. I hope that it will not be a missed opportunity. Negotiations have their ups and downs, but I believe that peace will be achieved. For Arabs and for Israelis, there is simply no better alternative.

Peace is essential to achieve our goal and maintain Israel as a state of the Jewish people, a democratic state, and a nation of growing excellence with an advanced and just society and a growing economy.

We now live in a new era. It is an era of rapid change. It is not the "new world order" that was predicted by some. Rather, it is a "new world disorder." Instead of a bipolar world, we now have, following the collapse of the Soviet Union, a multipolar world, led for the time being, by the only superpower, the United States.

Instead of capitalist-communist tension, we have ethnic, religious, and national unrest around the world.

We are also witnessing a new era in the Middle East. For Israel, this new era has opened up new opportunities. For the first time in the history of the Middle East, direct peace talks are being conducted between Israel and our neighboring Arab countries and the Palestinians. Yes, we are facing difficulties and hardships, but I believe it is an irreversible process.

At the same time, however, severe threats have developed: the proliferation of nuclear arms among nondemocratic countries . . . and the spread of the Islamic fundamentalist movement, led, supported, and financed by Iran.

But, on the other hand, the world has become more open to us following the end of the Cold War and the new approach of the government of Israel.

We have diplomatic relations with 125 of the 185 member states of the United Nations.

We have close relations with all five permanent members of the Security Council—the United States, the United Kingdom, France, Russia, and China.

When (and I say when and not if), peace will be achieved, we shall be able to divert more human energy and economic resources away from belligerency and conflict toward education, science, technological development, and human progress. Then Israel would become one of the most advanced economies and nations in the world.

But, of course, the main benefit will be a new quality of life and a better future for all peoples in the Middle East.

Now is perhaps a one–time historic opportunity to achieve peace.

I believe that the United States has a very significant role in helping the process. The United States was involved in the conclusion of the separation of forces between Israel, Egypt, and Syria in 1974; in the conclusion of the interim agreement between Israel and Egypt in 1975; the Camp David Accords in 1979; and in the formulation of Madrid Peace Conference in 1991.

Our goal is to maintain Israel as a democratic state and the homeland of the Jewish people.

For Israel, "To be or not to be" is not the question any more. Rather, it is: "What to be and how to be":

- a state of the Jewish people;
- a democratic state;
- a nation of excellence with a high quality of life.

I would like to conclude by stressing my strong conviction that the partnership between Israel and the Jewish people all over the world, the Diaspora Jewry, between you and us, is our backbone and source of strength.

I admire your work and devotion.

Thank you very much.

Excerpted from a speech delivered to NAAMAT-USA on 16 August 1993.

8

Holocaust and Heroism: The Lesson

The "Zionism–Racism" Libel

WE have come here tonight to mark the first anniversary of the revocation of the resolution that had equated Zionism with racism. For sixteen years, Resolution 3379 stood out as a blatant example of anti-Zionism and anti-Semitism. Its determination that Zionism was a form of racism was not only a miscarriage of justice, but also a miscarriage of truth and an abuse of the forum of the United Nations.

The revocation of that slander against the Jewish people was an important development for Israel but also for the United Nations itself. By revoking Resolution 3379, the international community was sending an important signal that expressions of hatred and intolerance are unacceptable to the enlightened nations of the world. Resolution 3379, as you all know, was passed on 10 November 1975, which was the thirty-seventh anniversary of Kristallnacht. How sadly ironic it is that today, as we mark the first anniversary of its revocation, the spectre of racism and neo-Nazism is once again on the rise in various countries all over the world.

Recently, there has been a wave of violent manifestations of racism and anti-Semitism. Hate crimes have targeted refugees, asylum seekers, foreigners, and others. In 1990, there were forty-six violent attacks against Jews, while in 1991 there were sixty-one attacks. Thus far, in 1992, there have been close to 100 such incidents, in addition to some 250 cases of threats, arson and damage to property. Across Europe, there are currently more than one thousand organizations with an anti-Semitic orientation.

Last Friday, I sent a letter to the UN Secretary General conveying the deep concern of the Government and people of Israel about the extensive racist, anti-Semitic, and xenophobic outbursts that have taken place recently. I also met with the President of the General Assembly, and I requested that he include a reference to the disturbing phenomena in his closing statement before the Assembly. On this important anniversary, as we mark the revocation of Resolution 3379, let us renew our commitment and redouble our efforts to fight racism and anti-Semitism in all its forms and wherever it appears. It is our duty and our mission to condemn this threat without hesitation and to put an end to it.

During the past week, there has been a spate of violent incidents in Israel, most recently the kidnapping and murder of Sgt. Major Nissim Toledano, whose body was found earlier today. Groups such as the fundamentalist Hamas are trying to kill Israelis and to kill the peace process as well. But we shall not surrender to the forces of terror. We shall not give in to those who are trying to violently derail the engine of peace. We are committed to the peace track. We are committed to the negotiations with our neighbors. Our quest for peace is sincere and determined. For that is the essence of Zionism: that the Jewish people should have a home where they can live in freedom, in democracy, in security, and in peace. And we shall never waver from this goal.

Address delivered to B'nai B'rith at a ceremony marking the first anniversary of the revocation of Resolution 3379, 15 December 1992.

Yom Hazikaron—Memorial Day for Israel's Fallen

We have come here today to remember. To remember and to commemorate the soldiers of the Israel Defense Forces and the security forces. To recall their heroism and their sacrifice, which brought about the establishment of the State of Israel. Their courage continues to sustain us. And their fortitude enables Israel to stand firm against any attempts to destroy her.

They physically defend the citizens of Israel, even as we speak. And they guard the reborn Jewish state that has arisen in the Land of Israel. As Lord Tennyson wrote, "I am a part of all that I have met; though much is taken, much abides. That which we are, we are; one equal temper of heroic hearts, strong in will, to strive, to seek, to find and not to yield."

As a result of their devotion, the State came into being. As a result of their contribution, Israel has been able to fulfill its historic role as a national home for the Jewish people. They have safeguarded the State, and enabled it to flower and to develop.

Our national drama continues to unfold. Israel has welcomed nearly half a million new immigrants from the former Soviet Union in the past four years. The Jewish population of Israel has grown sevenfold in the past four and a half decades. Our economy is thirty times larger than it was in 1948. Five hundred new Jewish towns and villages have been established. Our industry and science are among the most advanced in the world.

All this was achieved by Israel's citizens, both immigrants and sabras. All this was achieved with the backing and assistance of you—Jews who live outside of Israel. And it was achieved with the support of friendly countries around the world, especially the United States.

Above all, Israel owes its accomplishments to those young men and women who sacrificed everything. As the poet Rachel wrote, "It is a true covenant for us, an unbreakable bond; that which I have lost, it shall be my possession forever." Consolation will yet come. It will come from the great accomplishments and bright future that lie ahead of us.

It was Israel's strength that brought the Arab states and the Palestinians to direct negotiations for the first time in history.

Peace is also security. It will allow Israel to give expression to the excellence and quality of its people.

The key to economic development is peace. And the key to human development is peace. Once it is achieved, it will transform Israel into a great center of the Middle East and the Jewish people. In a recent letter addressed to the families of Israel's fallen servicemen, Prime Minister Rabin wrote as follows: "In the battle for peace, perhaps the last chapter of our wars, the memory of your sons and daughters . . . will accompany us." May their memory be for a blessing.

Address to Michigan Jewish community, 13 May 1993.

Yom Hashoah—Holocaust and Heroism Remembrance Day

Everyone is talking about the movie *Schindler's List.* But no one can fully grasp the enormity of the Shoah.

We know that 6 million Jews, 1.5 million of them children, were slaughtered by the Nazis and their collaborators. We know that the murderers systematically planned the genocide down to the smallest detail. But we will never understand how human beings—from what we like to think of as the "civilized" part of the world—can turn into inhuman monsters, how millions of people can lose their moral core.

On Yom HaShoah v'Hagvura, we remember not only the victims of Holocaust, but also the heroes of the Jewish resistance. In many cases, these people are one and the same. Despite almost insurmountable obstacles and no hope of victory, tens of thousands of Jews took up arms to fight the Nazis. In the ghettoes, in the forests, even in the camps.

The Vilna Ghetto was called the birthplace of armed Jewish resistance. There, the Jews organized the Farainigte Partizaner Organizatziah—the United Partisan Organization—which fought bravely despite the unbeatable odds. In May 1942, the ghetto fighters stole explosives and smuggled them through the underground tunnels below Vilna's Carmelite Monastery. They planted the explosives on nearby train tracks and blew up a German troop transport. The local peasants forced to clean up the wreckage and remains reported more than 200 Nazi soldiers dead.

Many of those who could not resist actively, resisted passively. The slogan of slave laborers in Nazi factories was "Work slowly!" Many went beyond that by sabotaging machinery and smuggling out weapons.

In 1942, the bitter Russian winter was taking its toll on tens of thousands of German soldiers. The Nazis needed winter clothing, so they forced Jews from the Vilna Ghetto to work as slave labor in the Kailis fur factory. But the Jewish workers resisted and burned down the factory. Nazi troops on the eastern front never got the sixty thousand sheepskin coats that were destroyed in the blaze.

Permit me another observation: Over the years, we have heard people, Americans and others, claim ignorance about what was happening to the Jews in Europe. "We didn't know," they said. But anyone who has visited the Holocaust Memorial Museum in Washington can see, in black and white, front page headlines from the *New York Times* and from other American newspapers from 1939 onward describing the unfolding Holocaust.

You can read about the Wannsee Conference of 20 January 1942, where the highest echelons of the Nazi death machine decided that their previous "solutions" to the "Jewish problem" were not enough. They decided upon a final solution to the problem, namely, to clean Europe of Jews through extermination. According to their calculations, eleven million people in all. The basic guideline of the

Final Solution—break the Jews' spirit before killing them, through degradation, terror, and deception.

Nothing in Europe was able to mobilize the United States to enter the war: not the threat of Nazi occupation of the entire continent. Not threat of German domination of Britain and the Soviet Union; and not the threat of mass extermination of every Jewish man, woman, and child in Europe. Only the bombing of Pearl Harbor in December 1941 by the Japanese led to United States involvement in World War II.

Once involved, American soldiers made a fateful contribution to defeat the Nazis and win the war. For that, we owe them our deepest gratitude and admiration.

But even though the Allies were fighting against the Nazis, they never bombed the death camps or the railroad tracks leading to them. Even something known as "trucks for blood" was rejected. This plan would have traded ten thousand trucks for the lives of one hundred thousand Hungarian Jews. But the British refused to supply the trucks that would have saved the Jews of Hungary.

Jews had little help from the outside. Hatred, apathy, and fear conspired to silence those who could have helped stop the slaughter. But there were the exceptions, the righteous among the nations—those who had not lost their humanity or their moral core. Oskar Schindler may be the most familiar to us now, but there are many other stories like his.

Georgio Perlasca saved thousands of Jews. An Italian wanted by his government, he managed to escape to Hungary, where he took a job in the Spanish embassy. When the Spanish envoy fled Budapest, Georgio started calling himself Jorge, and passed himself off as the new Spanish chargé d'affaires. No one suspected that he was actually an Italian on the run. In his new position, Perlasca issued Spanish papers to thousands of Jews and then demanded that the Fascist authorities respect the rights of all those under Spanish protection. He carried food and powdered milk to safe houses under the Spanish flag that sheltered hundreds of Jews. Many of these people were later able to flee Hungary by virtue of the Spanish papers he had given them.

After the war, two hundred thousand Jewish refugees were barred from entering British-controlled Palestine. They were turned away in multitudes, sent back to Europe and later Cyprus. The Jews of Palestine succeeded in smuggling in seventy thousand "illegal" immigrants between 1945 and 1948.

My mother and father came to Palestine in the early 1920s, but most of their family stayed in Ukraine and Byelorussia. I never had the good fortune to know them because none of them survived.

The Shoah is the traumatic memory of the Jewish people and a centerpiece of Israel's national consciousness. Our belief that we can rely only on ourselves stems in large measure from the harsh memory of the world's silence.

Because we rely on ourselves, we strive for excellence. For most of our short history, we have faced existential threats. Losing a war was never an option for us. So we invested in our people, our technology, our military, and our economy.

When we look around us today, we see the seeds of Nazism, which took root in the soil of anti-Semitism and amorality, scattered again throughout every corner of the world.

Recently, an important spokesman for a not insignificant American group called Jews "bloodsuckers," and invoked hateful slurs that serve as an invitation to racist violence. These slanders should be met with condemnation and complete opposition. Appeasing these people is a moral crime.

We all know the lesson the Shoah teaches about appeasing antisemitism. But there is another lesson, less well known, but equally important: Poles knew that the Jews in the Warsaw Ghetto were being slowly wiped out. Executions, deportations, degradation and starvation were no secrets. But to most citizens of Warsaw, Jewish lives had no value and Jewish death, no meaning. That changed when the Jews began to fight back.

On 20 April 1943, the Polish newspaper *Novy Dzen* described the revolt in the Warsaw Ghetto as it was happening. I quote: "The entire ghetto is a column of smoke, but in spite of this, the Jews continued their heroic, unyielding opposition. On several buildings, for example on the house at 4 Moranovska Street, the blue and white Zionist flag was raised, and alongside it, the flag of Poland."

In spirit, the heroes of the Jewish resistance during the Shoah were Israeli to the core. They embodied the Israeli ideal: Proud Jews, fearless defenders of their people, determined to live as free men and women, never to surrender.

A pamphlet circulated in the ghettoes in 1943 by the Fighting Pioneers read,

> We didn't have the privilege of actually participating in the building of our own land. . . . After we disappear, the Jews of Israel may be the only ones who will remember us, who will thrill with excitement and emotion at our deeds. Facing death, we unite ourselves with them in

their war of the future. Our every act is meant to clear the road for the freedom of the Jewish people . . .

Their deaths are our loss. As we remember their deeds today, may we all renew our own commitment to the ideals for which they lived and died.

Israel is the national and spiritual center of the Jewish people. The lesson of the Shoah attests to its historic importance. Israel has to pursue excellence, to pursue moral values. It must fulfill the prophetic injunction, "Seek peace and pursue it." It has to devote all of its resources—spiritual, economic, human—to build a greater future for the people of Israel and for every Jew willing to join us.

Address delivered to United Nations Judaica Book Club, 11 April 1994.

The Fiftieth Anniversary of the End of the World War Two

Commemorating the end of the World War Two is our moral obligation—not only to the fallen soldiers, but also to the civilian victims and to the honored veterans. It is also our obligation to the generations to come, so that they might learn from the past: The lessons of the World War Two are eternal lessons—always pertinent, always worthy of attention.

When we consider the bloodshed and slaughter that has taken place since the end of World War Two, we must ask if the world has fully learned the lessons of that war.

One of this century's greatest world leaders, Winston Churchill, once said, "An appeaser is one who feeds a crocodile, hoping it will eat him last." Appeasement and isolationism have not disappeared from the world. Rather, these sentiments have become loud and clear in many places. Such shortsightedness enabled fascism and Nazism to rise in the years before the World War Two. The terrible cost has to be a lesson for us all, especially today.

The price of appeasement, aggression and conflict in the World War Two is staggering. Tens of millions of soldiers and civilians dead, in the largest bloodbath in history. A generation of young men sacrificed. Cultural centers of the world—ravaged; the intelligentsia—massacred; art, architecture, beauty, and life—destroyed.

The war launched by the Nazis shattered the entire world and directed special fury against the Jewish people. Not only was the systematic annihilation of European Jewry unique in the history of the World War—it was, and remains, unique in the history of humankind. The Nazis mobilized every sector of society in a national effort to destroy all Jews. The government, the military, science, academia, business, the arts—all collaborated to first dehumanize and then destroy. The Nazis did not intend to conquer or enslave, but to annihilate an entire nation. Jews were murdered because they were Jews. They were guilty of nothing other than being born to Jewish parents. One of the survivors of the Holocaust, Elie Wiesel, put it best: "Not all victims were Jews. But all Jews were victims."

The years between 1939 and 1945 marked the final—and darkest—days of Jewish statelessness. The systematic extermination of the civilian Jewish populations of Nazi-occupied areas became one of the Nazis' main war goals. Six million Jews, one-third of the world's Jewish population, were wiped out.

The Jewish people's role in the World War Two was not only that of victim. Jewish soldiers joined in the fight against the Nazis. They fought—as Jews—in the Resistance armies and undergrounds all over Europe. Jews in Mandatory Palestine fought proudly in the Jewish Brigade of the British army. Those who were citizens of Allied countries fought as Russians, Americans, Canadians, British, French, and others.

We all owe a debt of honor and gratitude to the nations that fought to end the war, to liberate the occupied countries and to give new hope to the people and nations of the world. It was their finest hour. I hope that we all act in a manner befitting the memory of the millions who sacrificed their young lives to save others—to save humanity.

We have an obligation to build a world based on tolerance and mutual respect. But let us never be tolerant of fanaticism, fascism, or dictatorship. All these still plague the world today.

Our mission is perhaps greater than it was immediately following the end of the World War Two. We cannot change the past. But we can learn its lessons. We have responsibility to shape the future wisely. This has to be the outcome of the fiftieth anniversary commemoration.

The United Nations was established on the ruins of a world destroyed by hatred and violence, in order "to save succeeding generations from the scourge of war." The dangers of bigotry, prejudice, and discrimination are one of the enduring lessons of that dark period in human history. The United Nations has a special mission to ensure that such evil never rears its head again. As it carries out this task, may its member states always remember its roots, and may they faithfully chart its course into the future.

Excerpted from a speech delivered in the United Nations General Assembly, 2 December 1994.

The Lessons of the Second World War and the Holocaust

Israel has lent its support to the Russian initiative to commemorate the fiftieth anniversary of the end of the Second World War.

This is our moral obligation—not only to the fallen soldiers, to the civilian victims and to the honored veterans. It is also our obligation to the generations to come. The lessons of the Second World War are eternal: the evils of racism, the dangers of surrendering to despotism, the bankruptcy of appeasement, and the strength of statesmanship and courage.

I was born in the Land of Israel. But my parents came from Europe, where they both left behind large families. During the Second World War, over 50 members of my family, including two of my grandparents, were exterminated by the Nazis. As a child growing up in Israel I often wondered what I had missed by not knowing most of my family. As I became older, I understood that had my parents left Europe when they did, there is no doubt that their fates would have been the same as their families'.

But the survivors of the war have more bitter stories to tell. Many of them did not have the chance to know their parents, their brothers and sisters, their children.

For the State of Israel, the Second World War cannot be remembered without remembering the Holocaust—the systematic annihilation of six million Jewish people (1.5 million of them children) by the Nazis.

The war decimated European culture and civilization that had been nurtured for centuries. The war shattered the entire world. During their twelve-year reign of terror, the Nazis directed special fury against the Jewish people.

During these years the Jews of Europe were dehumanized and eventually destroyed. First they were stripped of all rights and dignity and rounded up into ghettos and separated from their countrymen. Starvation and disease hung over every Jewish ghetto. Death was a daily visitor.

As the war in Europe dragged on, the Nazis introduced their "Final Solution to the Jewish problem." Concentration camps and death camps were opened up throughout occupied Europe. It was in these camps that the Nazis attempted to extinguish the Jewish people as a whole.

The Nazis failed in their ultimate goal of eliminating the Jewish people from the community of nations. However, the years between 1939 and 1945 marked the destruction of Jewish life in Eastern and Central Europe. Two-thirds of European Jewry was obliterated in a total and systematic way. Communities rich in culture and spirit, commerce and science. Communities that gave the world Franz Kafka, Albert Einstein, Martin Buber, Primo Levy, and Karl Marx, were destroyed.

But the Holocaust is not only about the death of six million of our brothers and sisters. It is about the bravery and the heroism of the Jewish people in the face of horror. Many Jews chose to resist the Nazis. In the forests with the partisans. In the Warsaw ghetto. In the Treblinka death camp. And in countless other places. Jews condemned to death for the sole crime of being born Jewish faced their condemners and chose to die fighting. With dignity.

Jewish soldiers joined the fight against the Nazis. Wherever Partisans stood and fought, Jews stood with them. In Poland. In France. In Yugoslavia. In Russia.

I see a moral obligation to mention the brave individuals who risked their own lives to save the lives of others, both Jewish and non-Jewish. Schindler was not alone. There were righteous people in Holland, Denmark, Sweden, Norway, France, Poland, Italy, and other countries.

When the nightmare was over and the Nazis vanquished, it was the hope of Jewish sovereignty that sustained the survivors of the Nazi brutality. Upon war's end, the victorious allies set about the admirable goal of creating an international body that was committed to the cause of international peace and security and the establishment of a just society. Their efforts resulted in this United Nations, which today celebrates its fiftieth year.

Less than three years after the gas chambers ceased their operations, the UN passed the resolution on the partition of Palestine. This decision led directly to the birth of the State of Israel in May 1948. Since that time, Israel has become a home to hundreds of thousands of Holocaust survivors and their descendants. The State of Israel has become a haven for Jews fleeing persecution from around the world.

At times, I think that if Israel had existed before the Second World War, many of those who perished could have been saved.

We all owe a debt of honor and gratitude to the nations who

fought to end the war, to liberate the occupied countries and to give new hope to the people and nations of the world. It was their finest hour. I hope that we all act in a manner befitting the memory of the many millions who lost their lives to save others—to save humanity.

It is upon us all to remember the lessons of the Second World War and the Holocaust: the price of powerlessness and the evils of hatred and racism. Today, as we mark the victory of good over evil, of democracy over dictatorship, the specter of radicalism, racism, and hatred still loom over us all.

Today, the UN Member States have an obligation to build a world based on tolerance and mutual respect. We must not slacken in our fight against the poverty and hopelessness that creates fundamentalism and hatred. Our efforts must succeed.

The Jewish people can never forget the enormity of the Holocaust. The State of Israel, as the Jewish national home, has a special obligation to remember. An obligation to the memory of the six million who perished in the European graveyard. And an obligation to the survivors who have rebuilt their lives in Israel and elsewhere.

This resolution does not mention the Holocaust, but I must. For the six million whose voices have been forever silenced. For the Jewish people. For the State of Israel. And for future generations.

Excerpted from a speech delivered at the United Nations General Assembly on 18 October 1995.

Part Four
Culture and Excellence

9
Poetry and Peace

Writers and Artists for Peace in the Middle East

THIS evening is devoted not to the power politics in the world or in the Middle East. It has to do with art, spirit, and music.

In honor of Marvin Hamlisch, Wendy Wasserstein, and Shelly Winters, I would like to quote Heinrich Heine, a great German Jewish poet, on music: "Music is a marvel . . . a glimmering medium between mind and matter, related to both and yet differing from either. Spiritual and yet requiring rhythm; material and yet independent of space."

Can we live without art? without poetry? without music? Of course we can. But what kind of life would it be? Like a desert without a spring to drink water from. Like an ocean without waves or fish or ships.

On this, George Bernard Shaw said, "Without art, the crudeness of reality would make the world unbearable."

The Jewish people have given birth to a number of the greatest writers, artists, and thinkers in the annals of mankind, including Moses, the prophets Ezekiel, Jeremiah, Amos, and others, and the Song of Songs. We have given the world philosophers and authors such as Kafka, Spinoza, Heinrich Heine, Karl Marx, and Albert Einstein. More recently, we have been proud to count among our ranks men of stature such as Martin Buber, Isaiah Berlin, and some of the leading authors and historians of our time in the United States, Western and Eastern Europe, South America, and Israel.

The term *chosen people* has taken on an additional meaning: a nation of cultural and moral quality, a nation that has fashioned universal values in the fields of art, culture, and the spirit.

This was the secret of the continued survival of the Jewish people, despite the fact that we were deprived of a state for so many centuries. And this will be the key to our continued historical and spiritual existence. Israel, as the homeland of the Jewish people, must be the qualitative edge of this nation.

Israel will always be a small country from a quantitative point of view. But Israel's strength lies in her spiritual and intellectual quality, her scientific know-how, and her cultural creativity.

Israel began with agricultural settlement and then faced a military struggle for her very existence and has had to contest with massive waves of immigration. The time has come for Israel to turn her attention to scientific, cultural, and qualitative growth and development. Then the excellence of our people will again flourish and be expressed in a variety of beautiful colors, magnificent voices, and creative ideas and dreams.

The key elements are excellence, peace, democracy, and the opportunity for every member of our society to develop and express his virtues and potentials.

I believe that the substantial, the profound dilemma Israel is facing is not anymore "to be or not to be." The dilemma we are facing is what to be and how to be. Coping with this is our main challenge in the years to come. And the way to achieve it is peace, which is what this wonderful evening is all about.

Excerpted from a speech delivered to writers and artists for Middle East peace, 2 February 1993.

Education and Excellence: The Legacy of Yigal Allon

I've been fortunate to work with both Yitzhak Rabin and Yigal Allon. We served together in the cabinet from 1974–77, when Rabin was Prime Minister for the first time, and Allon was Minister of Foreign Affairs. I remember sitting as minister of Transportation in the special ministerial staff meetings, where we planned the Entebbe hostage rescue mission. I also remember the sensitivity Allon and Rabin showed to the human dimension. We didn't want to surrender to terrorism, but we also didn't want to endanger the hostages or soldiers. They gave serious thought to the question of how to protect human lives, even while standing up to terrorism and setting an example to the entire world. We succeeded to do both: We didn't surrender, and we saved the hostages. And we did all this with a minimum loss of life, 2,500 miles from home.

Yigal Allon was a role model for many in Israel. He believed that ethics should be central in politics. Allon died young, but accomplished much, and could have achieved much more had he lived. Born in the village Kfar Tavor in the Galilee, he became a member of kibbutz Ginnosar, the commander of the Palmach—the elite unit of the Jewish fighting force before the establishment of Israel, an army general, Knesset member, and government minister. As Minister of Education and Minister of Foreign Affairs, Allon sought to bring Israel into a new age of peace, security, and excellence. Already in 1968, he proposed what was later called the Allon Plan. This addressed the permanent settlement of the Israeli-Palestinian conflict by territorial compromise, based on security considerations.

Yitzhak Rabin has also devoted his life to Israel's peace and security. Born in Jerusalem, he became a Palmach commander, Israeli Army Chief of Staff during the Six Day War, Ambassador to Washington, Knesset member, Defense Minister and Prime Minister. Now, under his courageous leadership, we are working to achieve the true security that only peace can bring.

Of course, there are, and will be, ups and downs as we implement the agreement with the Palestinians. But we have to realize the simple truth: we can choose either painful compromise or perpetual conflict.

We still face difficulties as we make the agreement a reality. The enemies of peace, Iranian-backed terrorists such as Hizballah and Hamas, have targeted the peace process and its Arab and Israeli supporters.

Together with all responsible, moderate forces in the Middle East we shall fight terror with all our might, and we shall pursue peace with all our resolve.

We do believe that those who look to the future will prevail over those who are trapped in the past. I say this despite the painful violence and loss of human life during the past weeks. But I believe that all sides know that we have crossed the point of no return on our way to a new era of peace, security, economic cooperation, and social progress.

This is our obligation to future generations—to the young, to our children.

Peace will let us divert resources and energies away from conflict and toward education, health, and science. It will let us focus on absorbing the new immigrants. It will let us concentrate on economic development, improving the quality of life for all. And peace will let us expand our efforts to support universities, centers of learning, and culture.

Yigal Allon, for whom this prize is named, devoted his life to these goals. The Prime Minister of Israel, Yitzhak Rabin, is doing the same. Now, our dreams are closer to reality. I am proud to receive the Yigal Allon Prize on behalf of Prime Minister Rabin, and in his name and my own, I thank you.

Speech delivered at the Yigal Allon Award Dinner of the American Friends of the Open University, 13 December 1993.

Language, Poetry, and Politics

The Hebrew language, and with Jewish education are the two keys to maintaining the spiritual continuity of the Jewish people throughout the world—both in Israel and the Diaspora.

Language embodies a world of concepts and contains within it the most substantial elements of that which we call "culture." Language is no mere technical matter. It is a spiritual homeland, the well spring of a people's creativity. Especially for the Jewish people, which calls itself the People of the Book.

Words have power, and the Bible tells of the world's creation by the word of God: "Let there be light!" In Hebrew, "Yehi Or!" Two words. Some attribute to this metaphoric significance, others, historic or scientific. But I see in this a profound cultural significance for the Jewish people. Words can create. Words can destroy.

Language defines the internal meaning of a culture perhaps more than anything else. Take, for instance, the Hebrew word *midbar* ("desert"). A native Russian-speaker once told me that Russian has only one word to express this concept. In Hebrew, this concept can be expressed in many ways, *yeshimon, tziyah,* and so forth. In Arabic, there is a different word for every kind of desert, depending on the geographic conditions in which the word was formed.

In Hebrew, for example, there is no direct translation for two common English words: The first, "accountability," possibly because this is not a Hebrew concept. Scholars of the Hebrew language are searching for an appropriate term. So are politicians. They are also searching for a word to express what in English is called "integrity." Some use the term *yosher intellectuali* ("intellectual honesty"), but even this is not fully Hebrew.

Books and language have always been at the focus of Jewish life. But I fear what will happen when, one hundred years from now, biographers attempt to write the history of the great leaders of our day. Up until about fifty years ago, people generally left behind many letters, diaries, and writings that serve as a basis for reconstructing the past. For example, a firm foundation exists for anyone who wishes to write a biography of Ben-Gurion. He left behind a detailed diary—hour by hour—from age sixteen, letters, thousands of articles and speeches, and the recorded minutes of thousands of meetings. What will happen to the documenting of history when the entire business of state is conducted via telephone? Especially when here and there are "Watergates" large and small. Letter writing has almost passed from the world. Some articles remain, but we are mostly left with a few speeches and scattered interviews on CNN. In the foreseeable future, it will be harder to write a biography of prominent writers from our era than it will be to write on Tolstoy, who left behind tens of thousands of letters and diaries.

In Hebrew culture, the book remains the focus of cultural development. In the fifteenth century, the first printing press was not invented by Jews, but the first books printed were in Hebrew. This fact is significant. After all, the Hebrew language is not the tongue spoken by the majority of people in the world, and even then, it was the possession of but a tiny group that was a minority wherever it lived.

Political and poetic literature are stories unto themselves. Political literature serves also as an agent of struggle. If I may paraphrase the great Berthold Brecht, countless Jews and Israelis never stopped using their poetic voices, even when they became hoarse in the service of public, political, and national goals. Among those who figure most prominently in our consciousness is Bialik, whose poems often served public and political ends. Much of his work bears a message that has not lost its power or relevance, even today.

Literature's role as a weapon has a long history: It was simultaneously the means of dialogue and debate between priest and prophet, prophet and king, king and poet. Without a doubt, these relationships characterized the Jewish people throughout many periods of their history, including in the modern-day State of Israel and in the pre-state Yishuv that existed in Eretz Yisrael since the end of the nineteenth century.

To a certain extent, we see a reciprocal relationship with regard to politics as material for poetry and literature, and to poetry and literature as an agent of politics. Who does not remember the great author-activists who fought with the pen to attain the goals of political and national struggles. Vaclav Havel in Czechoslovakia; Beris Pasternak in Russia; in the United States, the songs of the Vietnam Era; the Irish poet Yeats—especially his poem "The Man and the Echo." He also wrote, by the way, one of the finest descriptions I have read of the distinction between politics and poetry: "From our quarrels with others we make rhetorics. From our quarrels with ourselves we make poetry."

In Israel, no less than among the Jewish people throughout its history, literature has served the national cause: poets like Slonksy, Uri Zvi Greenberg, and the younger generation—Nathan Zach, Yehuda Amichai, Dalia Ravikovitch, Haim Gouri. The poems of the War of Independence and the poems of the Lebanon War—all exemplify poetry in the service of political causes. They also exemplify the changes Israeli society has undergone in the past four and a half decades. Perhaps they even represent the battle for norms and values, fought by poets and authors with the pen as their weapon.

Many authors in Israel have put fine literature and poetry to the side to publish entire books that are essentially straightforward ideological polemics: Amos Oz's *In the Land of Israel,* A. B. Yehoshua's *Between Right and Right,* and *The Wall and the Mountain,* David Grossman's *The Yellow Wind* about Arabs in the territories, and also his new book on Arab-Israelis. Before them came many others like Yosef Chaim Brenner and Nathan Alterman, two of the giants of modern Hebrew literature.

But whereas Israeli literature has been drafted in support of political ends, we rarely see the converse phenomenon. Very little literature has been written by political leaders. In other nations it is more widespread—Per Almark, in Sweden, is a good example. Even in Israel, some authors have entered the political arena. This, however, usually only after they were well known as writers. By virtue of their writing, they entered into politics, and perhaps because of it, they also left: Yizhar Smilensky (S. Yizhar), Moshe Shamir, Uri Zvi Greenberg, Dov Seden. All were members of Knesset at one point or another. Shazar and Sharett also wrote, although they mainly focused their writings on political issues.

Politics and poetry are two different fields. And whoever tries to connect them can do this only through phonetics and only in English. Only two letters separate poetics from politics, but despite the phonetic proximity, the gulf between them is as wide as can be.

Politics is the art of the possible, the attempt to affect reality through direct means. Art, literature, and poetry are the acts of creating worlds whose boundaries are set by the artist and writer. In politics, the boundaries are set by what is possible. In art, the boundaries are set by the artist. This is an immense difference. It is all the difference in the world.

There is an inherent contradiction between the two realms, even if they come together sometimes in the same person. That person is marked by dualism.

Poetry is between a person and himself, a reflection of his relation to the outside world. Poetry is metaphoric. It is, in the end, the joint creation of the poet and the reader. A poem is a kaleidoscope in which the reader can see whatever he wants.

Politics is externalized, exposed—especially in Israel. The *homo politicus,* whose entire life is politics, will not write. The poet and author is, by definition, not *homo politicus.* Therefore, in the end, he will conclude his political life sooner or later.

For me, poetry has allowed me to maintain a balanced existence, even in times of intensive political activity. The impulse to write is a sharply felt need. Poetry springs from truth and is born of a seed that is hard to crack. I can explain how a poem is written from the technical side, as Gabriel Preil explained a few days ago that he writes on paper—not computer. He lets a poem "cool off" for two weeks. Some let it cool off for only one week, others, three months. But he couldn't explain, and maybe didn't want to, what metaphysical process was at work in the human soul. Association, impression, love, excitement, pain, identification—all bring forth a small seed that causes a poem to be written. All the rest is between me and myself and between me and the anonymous reader and who will read and write the poem anew.

Excerpted from a speech delivered to the Hebrew Association of America, and reprinted in Hadoar, 14 May 1993.

A Dream for Our Children

It is an honor for me to join in honoring Coretta Scott King and the memory of her husband, Dr. Martin Luther King, Jr.

Reverend King shared much in common with the Hebrew prophets who so inspired his life's work. The ancient prophets directed their words to their people, Israel. But their message of justice and righteousness was universal in scope. Micah said "What doth the Lord require of thee, but to do justly, and to love mercy, and to walk humbly with thy God?"

Martin Luther King, Jr. did justly. He worked to change America, to make his own country a better and more fair place. Yet his message of freedom and tolerance transcends national boundaries. It has gone forth from every mountainside in America to ring throughout the entire world. "No, no, we are not satisfied," he said, "and we will not be satisfied until justice rolls down like waters, and righteousness like a mighty stream." Gradually, his dream is being fulfilled here in the United States, in South Africa, and in countries on every continent. Still, much remains to be done.

King's legacy has touched many Jewish people here and in Israel, too. Many of us still remember the days before we regained our right to live in freedom. We remember how we suffered at the hands of people who did not believe that "All men are created equal." And so, we especially identify with the spirit and teachings of Martin Luther King, Jr.

Now, we are working with our neighbors to build a better future for the Middle East—to replace bloodshed with brotherhood. We, too, have a dream for our children—of peace, cooperation, dignity, and mutual respect.

But we are now in the midst of a struggle between those who look to the future and those who are trapped in the past. We will not be dragged back to the days of endless hatred and conflict. We have struck a new course and are determined to continue forward. Such was the vision of Martin Luther King, Jr. And especially at times like these, his legacy is an inspiration to us all.

Speech delivered to the World Jewish Congress commemoration of Martin Luther King, Jr. Day, 10 January 1995.

Appendix A: Significant Dates in Israeli-UN Relations

29 November 1947	Partition Plan for Palestine adopted by UN General Assembly.
14 May 1948	Israel declares independence.
11 May 1949	Israel admitted to United Nations.
22 November 1967	Security Council Resolution 242 adopted.
22 October 1973	Security Council Resolution 338 adopted.
1 September 1975	Israel-Egypt Interim Agreement reacted.
10 November 1975	"Zionism Is Racism" Resolution adopted by UN General Assembly.
17 September 1978	Camp David Accords signed with Egypt.
26 March 1979	Israel-Egypt Peace Treaty signed.
30 October 1991	Madrid Peace Conference convenes.
16 December 1991	"Zionism Is Racism" Resolution repealed by UN General Assembly.
13 September 1993	Israeli-Palestinian Declaration of Principles Signed.
14 December 1993	Positive resolution on Middle East peace process adopted.
4 May 1994	Gaza-Jericho Agreement signed with the PLO.
25 July 1994	Israel-Jordan Washington Declaration signed.
26 October 1994	Israel-Jordan Peace Treaty signed.
30 October 1994	First Middle East and North Africa Economic Summit convenes in Casablanca, Morocco.
28 September 1995	Interim Agreement (Oslo II) signed with the PLO.
29 October 1995	Second Middle East and North Africa Economic Summit convenes in Amman, Jordan.

Appendix B: The Partition Plan

Future Government of Palestine, General Assembly Resolution 181 (II), 29 November 1947:

The Ad-Hoc *Committee approved the proposal of Partition with Economic Union, and on 29 November the Assembly approved the plan, with 33 votes in favour, 13 against, 10 abstentions, and one absent. A United Nations Palestine Commission was established to supervise implementation of the Resolution under the guidance of the Security Council. Here is the breakdown of the vote:*

Yes: *Australia, Belgium, Bolivia, Brazil, Byelorussia, Canada, Costa Rica, Czechoslovakia, Denmark, Dominican Republic, Ecuador, France, Guatemala, Haiti, Iceland, Liberia, Luxembourg, Netherlands, New Zealand, Nicaragua, Norway, Panama, Paraguay, Peru, Philippines, Poland, Sweden, Ukraine, Union of South Africa, USSR, USA, Uruguay, Venezuela;*

No: *Afghanistan, Cuba, Egypt, Greece, India, Iran, Iraq, Lebanon, Pakistan, Saudi Arabia, Syria, Turkey, Yemen;*

Abstained: *Argentina, Chile, China, Colombia, El Salvador, Ethiopia, Honduras, Mexico, United Kingdom, Yugoslavia;*

Absent: *Siam.*

Following is the text of the Resolution:

The General Assembly

Having met in special session at the request of the mandatory Power to constitute and instruct a special committee to prepare for the consideration of the question of the future government of Palestine at the second regular session.

Having constituted a Special Committee and instructed it to investigate all questions and issues relevant to the problem of Palestine, and to prepare proposals for the solution of the problem, and

Having received and examined the report of the Special Committee (document A/364) including a number of unanimous recommendations and a plan of partition with economic union approved by the majority of the Special Committee.

Considers that the present situation in Palestine is one which is likely to impair the general welfare and friendly relations among nations;

Takes note of the declaration by the mandatory Power that it plans to complete its evacuation of Palestine by 1 August 1948;

Recommends to the United Kingdom, as the mandatory Power for Palestine, and to all other Members of the United Nations, the adoption and implementation, with regard to the future government of Palestine, of the Plan of Partition with Economic Union set out below;

Requests that

(a) The Security Council take the necessary measures as provided for in the plan for its implementation;

(b) The Security Council consider, if circumstances during the transitional period require such consideration, whether the situation in Palestine constitutes a threat to the peace. If it decides that such a threat exists, and in order to maintain international peace and security, the Security Council should supplement the authorization of the General Assembly by taking measures, under Articles 39 and 41 of the Charter, to empower the United Nations Commission, as provided in this resolution, to exercise in Palestine the functions which are assigned to it by this resolution.

(c) The Security Council determine as a threat to peace, breach of the peace or act of aggression, in accordance with Article 39 of the Charter, any attempt to alter by force the settlement envisaged by this resolution;

(d) The Trusteeship Council be informed of the responsibilities envisaged for it in this plan;

Calls upon the inhabitants of Palestine to take such steps as may be necessary on their part to put this plan into effect;

Appeals to all Governments and all peoples to refrain from taking any action which might hamper or delay the carrying out of these recommendations, and

Authorizes the Secretary-General to reimburse travel and subsistence expenses of the members of the Commission referred to in Part I, Section B, paragraph 1 below, on such basis and in such form as he may determine most appropriate in the circumstances, and to provide the Commission with the necessary staff to assist in carrying out the functions assigned to the Commission by the General Assembly.

The General Assembly

Authorizes the Secretary-General to draw from the Working Capital

Fund a sum not to exceed $2,000,000 for the purpose set forth in the last paragraph of the resolution on the future government of Palestine.

Plan of Partition with Economic Union

Part I. Future Constitution and Government of Palestine

A. *Termination of Mandate, Partition and Independence*

1. The Mandate for Palestine shall terminate as soon as possible but in any case not later than 1 August 1948.

2. The armed forces of the mandatory Power shall be progressively withdrawn from Palestine, the withdrawal to be completed as soon as possible but in any case not later than 1 August 1948.

The mandatory Power shall advise the Commission, as far in advance as possible, of its intention to terminate the Mandate and to evacuate each area.

The mandatory Power shall use its best endeavours to ensure that an area situated in the territory of the Jewish State, including a seaport and hinterland adequate to provide facilities for a substantial immigration, shall be evacuated at the earliest possible date and in any event not later than 1 February 1948.

3. Independent Arab and Jewish States and the Special International Regime for the City of Jerusalem, set forth in part III of this plan, shall come into existence in Palestine two months after the evacuation of the armed forces of the mandatory Power has been completed but in any case not later than 1 October 1948. The boundaries of the Arab State, the Jewish State, and the City of Jerusalem shall be as described in parts II and III below.

4. The period between the adoption by the General Assembly of its recommendation on the question of Palestine and the establishment of the independence of the Arab and Jewish States shall be a transitional period.

B. *Steps Preparatory to Independence*

1. A commission shall be set up consisting of one representative of each of five Member States. The Members represented on the Commission shall be elected by the General Assembly on as broad a basis, geographically and otherwise, as possible.

2. The administration of Palestine shall, as the mandatory Power withdraws its armed forces, be progressively turned over to the Commission, which shall act in conformity with the recommendations of the General Assembly, under the guidance of the Security Council. The mandatory Power shall to the fullest possible extent coordinate its plans for withdrawal with the plans of the Commission to take over and administer areas which have been evacuated.

In the discharge of this administrative responsibility, the Commission shall have authority to issue necessary regulations and take other measures as required.

The mandatory Power shall not take any action to prevent, obstruct or delay the implementation by the Commission of the measures recommended by the General Assembly.

3. On its arrival in Palestine the Commission shall proceed to carry out measures for the establishment of the frontiers of the Arab and Jewish States and the City of Jerusalem in accordance with the general lines of the recommendations of the General Assembly on the partition of Palestine. Nevertheless, the boundaries as described in part II of this plan are to be modified in such a way that village areas as a rule will not be divided by state boundaries unless pressing reasons make that necessary.

4. The Commission, after consultation with the democratic parties and other public organizations of the Arab and Jewish States, shall select and establish in each State as rapidly as possible a Provisional Council of Government. The activities of the Arab and Jewish Provisional Councils of Government shall be carried out under the general direction of the Commission.

If by 1 April 1948 a Provisional Council of Government cannot be selected for either of the states, or, if selected, cannot carry out its functions, the Commission shall communicate that fact to the Security Council for such action with respect to that State as the Security Council may deem proper, and to the Secretary-General for communication to the Members of the United Nations.

5. Subject to the provisions of these recommendations, during the transitional period the Provisional Councils of Government, acting under the Commission, shall have full authority in the areas under their control, including authority over matters of immigration and land regulation.

6. The Provisional Council of Government of each State, acting under the Commission, shall progressively receive from the Commission full responsibility for the administration of that State in the period between the termination of the Mandate and the establishment of the State's independence.

7. The Commission shall instruct the Provisional Council of Government of both the Arab and the Jewish States, after their formation, to proceed to the establishment of administrative organs of government, central and local.

8. The Provisional Council of Government of each State shall, within the shortest time possible, recruit an armed militia from the residents of that State, sufficient in number to maintain internal order and to prevent frontier clashes.

This armed militia in each State shall, for operational purposes, be under the command of Jewish or Arab officers resident in that State, but general political and military control, including the choice of the militia's High Command, shall be exercised by the Commission.

9. The Provisional Council of Government of each State shall, not later

than two months after the withdrawal of the armed forces of the mandatory Power, hold elections to the Constituent Assembly which shall be conducted on democratic lines. The election regulations in each state shall be drawn up by the Provisional Council of Government and approved by the Commission. Qualified voters for each State for this election shall be persons over eighteen years of age who are:

(a) Palestinian citizens residing in that State and

(b) Arabs and Jews residing in the State, although not Palestinian citizens, who, before voting, have signed a notice of intention to become citizens of such State.

Arabs and Jews residing in the City of Jerusalem who have signed a notice of intention to become citizens, the Arabs of the Arab State and the Jews of the Jewish State, shall be entitled to vote in the Arab and Jewish State respectively.

Women may vote and be elected to the Constituent Assemblies.

During the transitional period no Jew shall be permitted to establish residence in the area of the proposed Arab State, and no Arab shall be permitted to establish residence in the area of the proposed Jewish State, except by special leave of the Commission.

10. The Constituent Assembly of each State shall draft a democratic constitution for its State and choose a provisional government to succeed the Provisional Council of Government appointed by the Commission. The constitutions of the States shall embody chapters 1 and 2 of the Declaration provided for in Section C below and include *inter alia* provisions for:

(a) Establishing in each State a legislative body elected by universal suffrage and by secret ballot on the basis of proportional representation, and an executive body responsible to the legislature;

(b) Settling all international disputes in which the State may be involved by peaceful means in such a manner that international peace and security, and justice, are not endangered:

(c) Accepting the obligations of the State to refrain in its international relations from threat or use of force against the territorial integrity or political independence of any State, or in any other manner inconsistent with the purposes of the United Nations;

(d) Guaranteeing to all persons equal and non-discriminatory rights in civil, political, economic and religious matters and the enjoyment of human rights and fundamental freedoms, including freedom of religion, language, speech and publication, education, assembly and association;

(e) Preserving freedom of transit and visit for all residents and citizens of the other State in Palestine and the City of Jerusalem, subject to considerations of national security, provided that each State shall control residence within its borders.

11. The Commission shall appoint a preparatory economic commission of three members to make whatever arrangements are possible for economic cooperation, with a view to establishing, as soon as practicable, the

Economic Union and the Joint Economic Board, as provided in section D below.

12. During the period between the adoption of the recommendations on the question of Palestine by the General Assembly and the termination of the Mandate, the mandatory Power in Palestine shall maintain full responsibility for administration in areas from which it has not withdrawn its armed forces. The Commission shall assist the mandatory Power in the carrying out of these functions. Similarly, the mandatory Power shall cooperate with the Commission in the execution of its functions.

13. With a view to ensuring that there shall be continuity in the functioning of administrative services and that, on the withdrawal of the armed forces of the mandatory Power, the whole administration shall be in the charge of the Provisional Councils and the Joint Economic Board, respectively, acting under the Commission, there shall be a progressive transfer, from the mandatory Power to the Commission, of responsibility for all the functions of government, including that of maintaining law and order in the areas from which the forces of the mandatory Power have been withdrawn.

14. The Commission shall be guided in its activities by the recommendations of the General Assembly and by such instructions as the Security Council may consider necessary to issue.

The measures taken by the Commission, within the recommendations of the General Assembly, shall become immediately effective unless the Commission has previously received contrary instructions from the Security Council.

The Commission shall render periodic monthly progress reports, or more frequently, if desirable, to the Security Council.

15. The Commission shall make its final report to the next regular session of the General Assembly and to the Security Council simultaneously.

C. *Declaration*

A. A declaration shall be made to the United Nations by the provisional government of each proposed State before independence. It shall contain *inter alia* the following clauses:

The stipulations contained in the declaration are recognized as fundamental laws of the State and no law, regulation or official action shall conflict or interfere with these stipulations, nor shall any law, regulation or official action prevail over them.

Chapter 1. Holy Places, Religious Buildings and Sites

1. Existing rights in respect of Holy Places and religious buildings or sites shall not be denied or impaired.

2. In so far as Holy Places are concerned, the liberty of access, visit and transit shall be guaranteed, in conformity with existing rights, to all

residents and citizens of the other State and of the City of Jerusalem, as well as to aliens, without distinction as to nationality, subject to requirements of national security, public order and decorum. Similarly, freedom of worship shall be guaranteed in conformity with existing rights, subject to the maintenance of public order and decorum.

3. Holy Places and religious buildings or sites shall be preserved. No act shall be permitted which may in any way impair their sacred character. If at any time it appears to the Government that any particular Holy Place, religious building or site is in need of urgent repair, the Government may call upon the community or communities concerned to carry out such repair. The Government may carry it out itself at the expense of the community or communities concerned if no action is taken within a reasonable time.

4. No taxation shall be levied in respect of any Holy Place, religious building or site which was exempt from taxation on the date of the creation of the State.

No change in the incidence of such taxation shall be made which would either discriminate between the owners or occupiers of Holy Places, religious buildings or sites, or would place such owners or occupiers in a position less favourable in relation to the general incidence of taxation than existed at the time of the adoption of the Assembly's recommendations.

5. The Governor of the City of Jerusalem shall have the right to determine whether the provisions of the Constitution of the State in relation to Holy Places, religious buildings and sites within the borders of the State and the religious rights pertaining thereto, are being properly applied and respected, and to make decisions on the basis of existing rights in cases of disputes which may arise between the different religious communities or the rites of a religious community with respect to such places, buildings and sites. He shall receive full cooperation and such privileges and immunities as are necessary for the exercise of his functions in the State.

Chapter 2. Religious and Minority Rights

1. Freedom of conscience and the free exercise of all forms of worship, subject only to the maintenance of public order and morals, shall be ensured to all.

2. No discrimination of any kind shall be made between the inhabitants on the ground of race, religion, language or sex.

3. All persons within the jurisdiction of the State shall be entitled to equal protection of the laws.

4. The family law and personal status of the various minorities and their religious interests, including endowments, shall be respected.

5. Except as may be required for the maintenance of public order and good government, no measure shall be taken to obstruct or interfere with the enterprise of religious or charitable bodies of all faiths or to

discriminate against any representative or member of these bodies on the ground of his religion or nationality.

6. The State shall ensure adequate primary and secondary education for the Arab and Jewish minority respectively, in its own language and its cultural traditions.

The right of each community to maintain its own schools for the education of its own members in its own language, while conforming to such educational requirements of a general nature as the State may impose, shall not be denied or impaired. Foreign educational establishments shall continue their activity on the basis of their existing rights.

7. No restriction shall be imposed on the free use by any citizen of the State of any language in private intercourse, in commerce, in religion, in the Press or in publications of any kind, or at public meetings.

8. No expropriation of land owned by an Arab in the Jewish State (by a Jew in the Arab State) shall be allowed except for public purposes. In all cases of expropriation full compensation as fixed by the Supreme Court shall be paid previous to dispossession.

Chapter 3. Citizenship, International Conventions and Financial Obligations

1. *Citizenship.* Palestinian citizens residing in Palestine outside the City of Jerusalem, as well as Arabs and Jews who, not holding Palestinian citizenship, reside in Palestine outside the City of Jerusalem shall, upon the recognition of independence, become citizens of the State in which they are resident and enjoy full civil and political rights. Persons over the age of eighteen years may opt, within one year from the date of recognition of independence of the State in which they reside, for citizenship of the other State, providing that no Arab residing in the area of the proposed Arab State shall have the right to opt for citizenship in the proposed Jewish State and no Jew residing in the proposed Jewish State shall have the right to opt for citizenship in the proposed Arab State. The exercise of this right of option will be taken to include the wives and children under eighteen years of age of persons so opting.

Arabs residing in the area of the proposed Jewish State and Jews residing in the area of the proposed Arab State who have signed a notice of intention to opt for citizenship of the other State shall be eligible to vote in the elections to the Constituent Assembly of that State, but not in the elections to the Constituent Assembly of the State in which they reside.

2. *International Conventions. (a)* The State shall be bound by all the international agreements and conventions, both general and special, to which Palestine has become a party. Subject to any right of denunciation provided for therein, such agreements and conventions shall be respected by the State throughout the period for which they were concluded.

(b) Any dispute about the applicability and continued validity of international conventions or treaties signed or adhered to by the mandatory Power on behalf of Palestine shall be referred to the International Court of Justice in accordance with the provisions of the Statute of the Court.

3. *Financial Obligations. (a)* The State shall respect and fulfil all financial obligations of whatever nature assumed on behalf of Palestine by the mandatory Power during the exercise of the Mandate and recognized by the State. This provision includes the right of public servants to pensions, compensation or gratuities.

(b) These obligations shall be fulfilled through participation in the Joint Economic Board in respect of those obligations applicable to Palestine as a whole, and individually in respect of those applicable to, and fairly apportionate between, the States.

(c) A Court of Claims, affiliated with the Joint Economic Board, and composed of one member appointed by the United Nations, one representative of the United Kingdom and one representative of the State concerned, should be established. Any dispute between the United Kingdom and the State respecting claims not recognized by the latter should be referred to that Court.

(d) Commercial concessions granted in respect of any part of Palestine prior to the adoption of the resolution by the General Assembly shall continue to be valid according to their terms, unless modified by agreement between the concession-holders and the State.

Chapter 4. Miscellaneous Provisions

1. The provisions of chapters 1 and 2 of the declaration shall be under the guarantee of the United Nations, and no modifications shall be made in them without the assent of the General Assembly of the United Nations. Any Member of the United Nations shall have the right to bring to the attention of the General Assembly any infraction or danger of infraction of any of these stipulations, and the General Assembly may thereupon make such recommendations as it may deem proper in the circumstances.

2. Any dispute relating to the application or interpretation of this declaration shall be referred, at the request of either party, to the International Court of Justice, unless the parties agree to another mode of settlement.

D. *Economic Union and Transit*

1. The Provisional Council of Government of each State shall enter into an undertaking with respect to Economic Union and Transit. This undertaking shall be drafted by the Commission provided for in Section B, paragraph 1, utilizing to the greatest possible extent the advice and cooperation of representative organizations and bodies from each of the proposed States. It shall contain provisions to establish the Economic Union of Palestine and provide for other matters of common interest. If by 1 April 1948 the Provisional Councils of Government have not entered into the undertaking, the undertaking shall be put into force by the Commission.

The Economic Union of Palestine

2. The objectives of the Economic Union of Palestine shall be:

(*a*) A customs union;
(*b*) A joint currency system providing for a single foreign exchange rate;
(*c*) Operation in the common interest on a non-discriminatory basis of railways; inter-State highways; postal, telephone and telegraphic services and ports and airports involved in international trade and commerce;
(*d*) Joint economic development, especially in respect of irrigation, land reclamation and soil conservation;
(*e*) Access for both States and for the City of Jerusalem on a non-discriminatory basis to water and power facilities.

3. There shall be established a Joint Economic Board, which shall consist of three representatives of each of the two States and three foreign members appointed by the Economic and Social Council of the United Nations. The foreign members shall be appointed in the first instance for a term of three years; they shall serve as individuals and not as representatives of States.

4. The functions of the Joint Economic Board shall be to implement either directly or by delegation the measures necessary to realize the objectives of the Economic Union. It shall have all powers of organization and administration necessary to fulfil its functions.

5. The States shall bind themselves to put into effect the decisions of the Joint Economic Board. The Board's decisions shall be taken by a majority vote.

6. In the event of failure of a State to take the necessary action the Board may, by a vote of six members, decide to withhold an appropriate portion of the part of the customs revenue to which the State in question is entitled under the Economic Union. Should the State persist in its failure to cooperate, the Board may decide by a simple majority vote upon such further sanctions, including disposition of funds which it has withheld, as it may deem appropriate.

7. In relation to economic development, the functions of the Board shall be planning, investigation and encouragement of joint development projects, but it shall not undertake such projects except with the assent of both States and the City of Jerusalem, in the event that Jerusalem is directly involved in the development project.

8. In regard to the joint currency system, the currencies circulating in the two States and the City of Jerusalem shall be issued under the authority of the joint Economic Board, which shall be the sole issuing authority and which shall determine the reserves to be held against such currencies.

9. So far as is consistent with paragraph 2(*b*) above, each State may operate its own central bank, control its own fiscal and credit policy, its

foreign exchange receipts and expenditures, the grant of import licenses, and may conduct international financial operations on its own faith and credit. During the first two years after the termination of the Mandate, the Joint Economic Board shall have the authority to take such measures as may be necessary to ensure that—to the extent that the total foreign exchange revenues of the two States from the export of goods and services permit, and provided that each State takes appropriate measures to conserve its own foreign exchange resources—each State shall have available, in any twelve months' period, foreign exchange sufficient to assure the supply of quantities of imported goods and services for consumption in its territory equivalent to the quantities of such goods and services consumed in that territory in the twelve months' period ending 31 December 1947.

10. All economic authority not specifically vested in the Joint Economic Board is reserved to each State.

11. There shall be a common customs tariff with complete freedom of trade between the States, and between the States and the City of Jerusalem.

12. The tariff schedules shall be drawn up by a Tariff Commission, consisting of representatives of each of the States in equal numbers, and shall be submitted to the Joint Economic Board for approval by a majority vote. In case of disagreement in the Tariff Commission, the Joint Economic Board shall arbitrate the points of difference. In the event that the Tariff Commission fails to draw up any schedule by a date to be fixed, the Joint Economic Board shall determine the tariff schedule.

13. The following items shall be a first charge on the customs and other common revenue of the Joint Economic Board:

(a) The expenses of the customs service and of the operation of the joint services;

(b) The administrative expenses of the Joint Economic Board;

(c) The financial obligations of the Administration of Palestine, consisting of:

i The service of the outstanding public debt;

ii The cost of superannuation benefits, now being paid or falling due in the future, in accordance with the rules and to the extent established by paragraph 3 of chapter 3 above.

14. After these obligations have been met in full, the surplus revenue from the customs and other common services shall be divided in the following manner: not less than 5 per cent and not more than 10 per cent to the City of Jerusalem; the residue shall be allocated to each State by the Joint Economic Board equitably, with the objective of maintaining a sufficient and suitable level of government and social services in each State, except that the share of either State shall not exceed the amount of that State's contribution to the revenues of the Economic Union by more than approximately four million pounds in any year. The amount

granted may be adjusted by the Board according to the price level in relation to the prices prevailing at the time of the establishment of the Union. After five years, the principles of the distribution of the joint revenue may be revised by the Joint Economic Board on a basis of equity.

15. All international conventions and treaties affecting customs tariff rates, and those communications services under the jurisdiction of the Joint Economic Board, shall be entered into by both States. In these matters, the two States shall be bound to act in accordance with the majority of the Joint Economic Board.

16. The Joint Economic Board shall endeavour to secure for Palestine's exports fair and equal access to world markets.

17. All enterprises operated by the Joint Economic Board shall pay fair wages on a uniform basis.

Freedom of Transit and Visit

18. The undertaking shall contain provisions preserving freedom of transit and visit for all residents or citizens of both States and of the City of Jerusalem, subject to security considerations; provided that each State and the City shall control residence within its borders.

19. The undertaking and any treaty issuing therefrom shall remain in force for a period of ten years. It shall continue in force until notice of termination, to take effect two years thereafter, is given by either of the parties.

20. During the initial ten-year period, the undertaking and any treaty issuing therefrom may not be modified except by consent of both parties and with the approval of the General Assembly.

21. Any dispute relating to the application or the interpretation of the undertaking and any treaty issuing therefrom shall be referred, at the request of either party, to the International Court of Justice, unless the parties agree to another mode of settlement.

E. *Assets*

1. The movable assets of the Administration of Palestine shall be allocated to the Arab and Jewish States and the City of Jerusalem on an equitable basis. Allocations should be made by the United Nations Commission referred to in section B, paragraph 1, above. Immovable assets shall become the property of the government of the territory in which they are situated.

2. During the period between the appointment of the United Nations Commission and the termination of the Mandate, the mandatory Power shall, except in respect of ordinary operations, consult with the Commission on any measure which it may contemplate involving the liquidation, disposal or encumbering of the assets of the Palestine Government, such as the accumulated treasury surplus, the proceeds of Government bond issues, State lands or any other asset.

F. *Admission to Membership in the United Nations*

When the independence of either the Arab or the Jewish State as envisaged in this plan has become effective and the declaration and undertaking, as envisaged in this plan, have been signed by either of them, sympathetic consideration should be given to its application for admission to membership in the United Nations in accordance with article 4 of the Charter of the United Nations.

Part II. Boundaries

A. *The Arab State*

The area of the Arab State in Western Galilee is bounded on the west by the Mediterranean and on the north by the frontier of the Lebanon from Ras en Naqura to a point north of Saliha. From there the boundary proceeds southwards, leaving the built-up area of Saliha in the Arab State, to join the southernmost point of this village. There it follows the western boundary line of the villages of 'Alma, Rihaniya and Teitaba, thence following the northern boundary line of Meirun village to join the Acre-Safad sub-district boundary line. It follows this line to a point west of Es Sammu'i village and joins it again at the northernmost point of Farradiya. Thence it follows the sub-district boundary line to the Acre-Safad main road. From here it follows the western boundary of Kafr I'nan village until it reaches the Tiberias-Acre sub-district boundary line, passing to the west of the junction of the Acre-Safad and Lubiya-Kafr I'nan roads. From the southwest corner of Kafr I'nan village the boundary line follows the western boundary of the Tiberias sub-district to a point close to the boundary line between the villages of Maghar and Eilabun, then bulging out to the west to include as much of the eastern part of the plain of Battuf as is necessary for the reservoir proposed by the Jewish Agency for the irrigation of lands to the south and east.

The boundary rejoins the Tiberias sub-district boundary at a point on the Nazareth-Tiberias road southeast of the built-up area Tur'an; thence it runs southwards, at first following the sub-district boundary and then passing between the Kadoorie Agricultural School and Mount Tabor, to a point due south at the base of Mount Tabor. From here it runs due west, parallel to the horizontal grid line 230, to the north-east corner of the village lands of Tel Adashim. It then runs to the north-west corner of these lands, whence it turns south and west so as to include in the Arab State the sources of the Nazareth water supply in Yafa village. On reaching Ginneiger it follows the eastern, northern and western boundaries of the lands of this village to their south-west corner, whence it proceeds in a straight line to a point on the Haifa-Afula Railway on the boundary between the villages of Sarid and El Mudeidil. This is the point of intersection.

The south-western boundary of the area of the Arab State in Galilee takes a line from this point, passing northwards along the eastern boundaries of Sarid and Gevat to the north-eastern corner of Nahalal, proceeding thence across the land of Kefar ha Horesh to a central point on the southern boundary of the village of 'Illut, thence westwards along that village boundary to the eastern boundary of Beit Lahm, thence northwards and north-eastwards along its western boundary to the north-eastern corner of Waldheim and thence north-westwards across the village lands Shafa 'Amr to the south-eastern corner of Ramat Yohanan. From here it runs due north-north-east to a point on the Shafa 'Amr-Haifa road, west of its junction with the road to I'Billin. From there it proceeds north-east to a point on the southern boundary of I'Billin situated to the west of the I'Billin-Birwa road. Thence along that boundary to its westernmost point, whence it turns to the north, follows across the village land of Tamra to the north-westernmost corner and along the western boundary of Julis until it reaches the Acre-Safad road. It then runs westward along the southern side of the Safad-Acre road to the Galilee-Haifee District boundary, from which point it follows that boundary to the sea.

The boundary of the hill country of Samaria and Judea starts on the Jordan River at the Wadi Malih south-east of Beisan and runs due west to meet the Beisan-Jericho road and then follows the western side of that road in a north-westerly direction to the junction of the boundaries of the sub-districts of Beisan, Nablus and Jenin. From that point it follows the Nablus-Jenin sub-district boundary westwards for a distance of about three kilometres and then turns north-westwards, passing to the east of the built-up areas of the villages of Jalbun and Faqqu'a, to the boundary of the sub-districts of Jenin and Beisan at a point north-east of Nuris. Thence it proceeds first north-westwards to a point due north of the built-up area of Zie'in and then westwards to the Afula-Jenin railway, thence north-westwards along the district boundary line to the point of intersection on the Hejaz railway. From here the boundary runs south-westwards, including the built-up area and some of the land of the village of Kh. Lid in the Arab State to cross the Haifa-Jenin road at a point on the district boundary between Haifa and Samaria west of El Mansi. It follows this boundary to the southern-most point of the village of El Buteimat. From here it follows the northern and eastern boundaries of the village of Ar'ara, rejoining the Haifa-Samaria district boundary at Wadi'Ara, and thence proceeding south-south-westwards in an approximately straight line joining up with the western boundary of Qaqun to a point east of the railway line on the eastern boundary of Qaqun village. From here it runs along the railway line some distance to the east of it to a point just east of the Tulkarm railway station. Thence the boundary follows a line halfway between the railway and the Tulkarm-Qalqilya-Jaljuliya and Ras el Ein road to a point just east of Ras El Ein station, whence it proceeds along the railway some distance to the east of it to the point on the railway line south of the junction of the Haifa-Lydda and Beit Nabala lines, whence it proceeds along the southern border of Lydda airport to its south-west corner, thence in a south-westerly direction to a point just west of the built-up area of Sarafand el Amar, whence it turns south, passing just to the west of the built-up area of Abu el Fadil to the northeast corner of the lands of Beer Ya'aqov. (The boundary line should be so demarcated as to allow direct access from the Arab State to the airport.) Thence the boundary line follows the western and southern boundaries of Ramle village, to the north-east corner of El Na'ana village, thence in a straight line to the southernmost point of El Barriya, along the eastern boundary of that village and the southern boundary of 'Innaba village. Thence it turns north to follow the southern side of the Jaffa-Jerusalem road until El Qubab, whence it follows the road to the boundary of Abu Shusha. It runs along the eastern boundaries of Abu Shusha, Seidun, Hulda to the southernmost point of Hulda, thence westwards in a straight line to the north-eastern corner of Umm Kalkha, thence following the northern boundaries of Umm Kalkha, Qazaza and the northern and western boundaries of Mukhezin to the Gaza District boundary and thence runs across the village lands of El Mismiya, El Kabira, and Yasur to the southern point of intersection, which is midway between the built-up areas of Yasur and Batani Sharqi.

From the southern point of intersection the boundary lines run north-westwards between the villages of Gan Yavne and Barqa to the sea at a point half way between Nabi Yunis and Minat el Qila, and south-eastwards to a point west of Qastina, whence it turns in a south-westerly direction, passing to the east of the built-up areas of Es Sawafir, Esh Sharqiya and Ibdis. From the south-east corner of Ibdis village it runs to a point south-west of the built-up area of Beit'Affa, crossing the Hebron-El Majdal road just to the west of the built-up area of Iraq Suweidan. Thence it proceeds southwards along the western village boundary of El Faluja to the Beersheba sub-district boundary. It then runs across the tribal lands of 'Arab el Jubarat to a point on the boundary between the sub-districts of Beersheba and Hebron north of Kh. Khuweilifa, whence it proceeds in a south-westerly direction to a point on the Beersheba-Gaza main road two kilometres to the north-west of the town. It then turns south-eastwards to reach Wadi Sab' at a point situated one kilometre to the west of it. From here it turns north-eastwards and proceeds along Wadi Sab' and along the Beersheba-Hebron road for a distance of one kilometre, whence it turns eastwards and runs in a straight line to Kh. Kuseifa to join the Beersheba-Hebron sub-district boundary. It then follows the Beersheba-Hebron boundary eastwards to a point north of Ras Ez Zurire, only departing from it so as to cut across the base of the indentation between vertical grid lines 150 and 160.

About five kilometres north-east of Ras Ez Zuweira it turns north, excluding from the Arab State a strip along the coast of the Dead Sea not more than seven kilometres in depth, as far as Ein Geddi, whence it turns due east to join the Transjordan frontier in the Dead Sea.

The northern boundary of the Arab section of the coastal plain runs from a point between Minat el Qila and Nabi Yunis, passing between the built-up areas of Gan Yavne and Barqa to the point of intersection. From here it turns south-westwards, running across the lands of Batani Sharqi, along the eastern boundary of the lands of Beit Daras and across the lands of Julis, leaving the built-up areas of Batani Sharqi and Julis to the westwards, as far as the north-west corner of the lands of Beit Tima. Thence it runs east of El Jiya across the village lands of El Barbara along the eastern boundaries of the villages of Beit Jirja, Deir Suneid and Dimra. From the south-east corner of Dimra the boundary passes across the lands of Beit Hanun leaving the Jewish lands of Nir-Am to the eastwards. From the south-east corner of Beit Hanun the line runs south-west to a point south of the parallel grid line 100, then turns north-west for two kilometres turning again in a south-westerly direction and continuing in an almost straight line to the north-west corner of the village lands of Kirbet Ikhza'a. From there it follows the boundary line of this village to its southernmost point. It then runs in a southerly direction along the vertical grid line 90 to its junction with the horizontal grid line 70. It then turns south-eastwards to Kh. el Ruheiba and proceeds in a southerly direction to a point known as El Baha, beyond which crosses the Beersheba-El Auja main road to the west of Kh. el Mushrifa. From there it joins Wadi El Zaiyatin just to the west of El Subeita. From there it turns to the north-east and then to south-east following this wadi and passes to the east of 'Abda to join Wadi Nafkh. It then bulges to the south-west along Wadi Nakkh, Wadi Ajrim and Wadi Lassan to the point where Wadi Lassan crosses the Egyptian frontier.

The area of the Arab enclave of Jaffa consists of that part of the town-planning area of Jaffa which lies to the west of the Jewish quarters lying south of Tel-Aviv, to the west of the continuation of Herzl street up to its junction with the Jaffa-Jerusalem road, to the south-west of the section of the Jaffa-Jerusalem road lying south-east of that junction, to the west of Miqve Yisrael lands, to the north-west of Holon local council, to the north of the line linking up the north-west corner of Holon with the north-east corner of Bat-Yam local council area and to the north of Bat-Yam local council area. The question of Karton quarters will be decided by the Boundary Commission, bearing in mind among other considerations the desirability of including the smallest number of its Arab inhabitants and the largest possible number of its Jewish inhabitants in the Jewish State.

B. *The Jewish State*

The north-eastern sector of the Jewish State (Eastern Galilee) is bounded on the north and west by the Lebanese frontier and on the east by the frontiers of Syria and Transjordan. It includes the whole of the Hula Basin, Lake Tiberias, the whole of the Beisab sub-district, the boundary line being extended to the crest of the Gilboa mountains and the Wadi

Malih. From there the Jewish State extends north-west, following the boundary described in respect of the Arab State.

The Jewish section of the coastal plain extends from a point between Minat el Qila and Nabi Yunis in the Gaza sub-district and includes the towns of Haifa and Tel Aviv, leaving Jaffa as an enclave of the Arab State. The eastern frontier of the Jewish State follows the boundary described in respect of the Arab State.

The Beersheba area comprises the whole of the Beersheba sub-district, including the Negeb and the eastern part of the Gaza sub-district, but excluding the town of Beersheba and those areas described in respect of the Arab State. It includes also a strip of land along the Dead Sea stretching from the Beersheba-Hebron sub-district boundary line to Ein Geddi, as described in respect of the Arab State.

C. *The City of Jerusalem*

The boundaries of the City of Jerusalem are as defined in the recommendations on the City of Jerusalem (See Part III, Section B, below).

Part III. City of Jerusalem

A. *A Special Regime*

The City of Jerusalem shall be established as a *corpus separatum* under a special international regime and shall be administered by the United Nations. The Trusteeship Council shall be designated to discharge the responsibilities of the Administering Authority on behalf of the United Nations.

B. *Boundaries of the City*

The City of Jerusalem shall include the present municipality of Jerusalem plus the surrounding villages and towns, the most eastern of which shall be Abu Dis; the most southern, Bethlehem; the most western, Ein Karim (including also the built-up area of Motsa); and the most northern Shu'fat, as indicated on the attached sketch-map (annex B).

C. *Statute of the City*

The Trusteeship Council shall, within five months of the approval of the present plan, elaborate and approve a detailed Statute of the City which shall contain *inter alia* the substance of the following provisions:

1. *Government Machinery; Special Objectives.* The Administering Authority in discharging its administrative obligations shall pursue the following special objectives;

(a) To protect and to preserve the unique spiritual and religious interests located in the city of the three great monotheistic faiths throughout

the world, Christian, Jewish and Moslem; to this end to ensure that order and peace, and especially religious peace, reign in Jerusalem.

(b) To foster cooperation among all the inhabitants of the city in their own interests as well as in order to encourage and support the peaceful development of the mutual relations between the two Palestinian peoples throughout the Holy Land; to promote the security, well-being and any constructive measures of development of the residents, having regard to the special circumstances and customs of the various people and communities.

2. *Governor and Administrative Staff.* A Governor of the City of Jerusalem shall be appointed by the Trusteeship Council and shall be responsible to it. He shall be selected on the basis of special qualifications and without regard to nationality. He shall not, however, be a citizen of either State in Palestine.

The Governor shall represent the United Nations in the City and shall exercise on their behalf all powers of administration, including the conduct of external affairs. He shall be assisted by an administrative staff classed as international officers in the meaning of Article 100 of the Charter and chosen whenever practicable from the residents of the city and of the rest of Palestine on a non-discriminatory basis. A detailed plan for the organization of the administration of the city shall be submitted by the Governor to the Trusteeship Council and duly approved by it.

3. *Local Autonomy.*

(a) The existing local autonomous units in the territory of the city (villages, townships and municipalities) shall enjoy wide powers of local government and administration.

(b) The Governor shall study and submit for the consideration and decision of the Trusteeship Council a plan for the establishment of special town units consisting, respectively, of the Jewish and Arab sections of Jerusalem. The new town units shall continue to form part of the present municipality of Jerusalem.

4. *Security Measures.*

(a) The City of Jerusalem shall be demilitarized; its neutrality shall be declared and preserved and no para-military formations, exercises or activities shall be permitted within its borders.

(b) Should the administration of the City of Jerusalem be seriously obstructed or prevented by the non-cooperation or interference of one or more sections of the population, the Governor shall have the authority to take such measures as may be necessary to restore the effective functioning of the administration.

(c) To assist in the maintenance of internal law and order and especially for the protection of the Holy Places and religious buildings and sites in the city, the Governor shall organize a special police force of adequate strength, the members of which shall be recruited outside of Palestine. The Governor shall be empowered to direct such budgetary provision as may be necessary for the maintenance of this force.

5. *Legislative Organization.* A Legislative Council, elected by adult residents of the City irrespective of nationality on the basis of universal and secret suffrage and proportional representation, shall have powers of legislation and taxation. No legislative measures shall, however, conflict or interfere with the provisions which will be set forth in the Statute of the City, nor shall any law, regulation or official action prevail over them. The Statute shall grant to the Governor a right of vetoing bills inconsistent with the provisions referred to in the preceding sentence. It shall also empower him to promulgate temporary ordinances in case the Council fails to adopt a bill deemed essential to the normal functioning of the administration.

6. *Administration of Justice.* The Statute shall provide for the establishment of an independent judiciary system, including a court of appeal. All the inhabitants of the City shall be subject to it.

7. *Economic Union and Economic Regime.* The City of Jerusalem shall be included in the Economic Union of Palestine and be bound by all stipulations of the undertaking and of any treaties issued therefrom, as well as by the decisions of the Joint Economic Board. The Headquarters of the Economic Board shall be established in the territory of the City.

The Statute shall provide for the regulation of economic matters not falling within the regime of the Economic Union, on the basis of equal treatment and non-discrimination for all Members of the United Nations and their nationals.

8. *Freedom of Transit and Visit; Control of Residents.* Subject to considerations of security, and of economic welfare as determined by the Governor under the directions of the Trusteeship Council, freedom of entry into, and residence within, the borders of the City shall be guaranteed for the residents or citizens of the Arab and Jewish States. Immigration into, and residence within, the borders of the City for nationals of other States shall be controlled by the Governor under the directions of the Trusteeship Council.

9. *Relations with the Arab and Jewish States.* Representatives of the Arab and Jewish States shall be accredited to the Governor of the City and charged with the protection of the interests of their States and nationals in connection with the international administration of the City.

10. *Official Languages.* Arabic and Hebrew shall be the official languages of the city. This will not preclude the adoption of one or more additional working languages, as may be required.

11. *Citizenship.* All the residents shall become *ipso facto* citizens of the City of Jerusalem unless they opt for citizenship of the State of which they have been citizens, or, if Arabs or Jews, have filed notice of intention to become citizens of the Arab or Jewish State respectively, according to Part I, Section B, Paragraph 9, of this plan.

The Trusteeship Council shall make arrangements for consular protection of the citizens of the City outside its territory.

12. *Freedoms of Citizens.*

(a) Subject only to requirements of public order and morals, the inhabitants of the City shall be ensured the enjoyment of human rights and fundamental freedoms, including freedom of conscience, religion and worship, language, education, speech and press, assembly and association, and petition.

(b) No discrimination of any kind shall be made between the inhabitants on the grounds of race, religion, language or sex.

(c) All persons within the City shall be entitled to equal protection of the laws.

(d) The family law and personal status of the various persons and communities and their religious interests, including endowments, shall be respected.

(e) Except as may be required for the maintenance of public order and good government, no measure shall be taken to obstruct or interfere with the enterprise of religious or charitable bodies of all faiths or to discriminate against any representative or member of these bodies on the ground of his religion or nationality.

(f) The City shall ensure adequate primary and secondary education for the Arab and Jewish communities respectively, in their own languages and in accordance with their cultural traditions.

The right of each community to maintain its own schools for the education of its own members in its own language, while conforming to such educational requirements of a general nature as the City may impose, shall not be denied or impaired. Foreign educational establishments shall continue their activity on the basis of their existing rights.

(g) No restriction shall be imposed on the free use by any inhabitant of the City of any language in private intercourse, in commerce, in religion, in the Press or in publications of any kind, or at public meetings.

13. *Holy Places*

(a) Existing rights in respect of Holy Places and religious buildings or sites shall not be denied or impaired.

(b) Free access to the Holy Places and religious buildings or sites and the free exercise of worship shall be secured in conformity with existing rights and subject to the requirements of public order and decorum.

(c) Holy Places and religious buildings or sites shall be preserved. No act shall be permitted which may in any way impair their sacred character. If at any time it appears to the Governor that any particular Holy Place, religious building or site is in need of urgent repair, the Governor may call upon the community or communities concerned to carry out such repair. The Governor may carry it out himself at the expense of the community or communities concerned if no action is taken within a reasonable time.

(d) No taxation shall be levied in respect of any Holy Place, religious building or site which was exempt from taxation on the date of the creation of the City. No change in the incidence of such taxation shall be made which would either discriminate between the owners or occupiers

of Holy Places, religious buildings or sites, or would place such owners or occupiers in a position less favourable in relation to the general incidence of taxation than existed at the time of the adoption of the Assembly's recommendations.

14. *Special powers of the Governor* in respect of the Holy Places, religious buildings and sites in the City and in any part of Palestine.

(a) The protection of the Holy Places, religious buildings and sites located in the City of Jerusalem shall be a special concern of the Governor.

(b) With relation to such places, buildings and sites in Palestine outside the city, the Governor shall determine on the ground of powers granted to him by the Constitutions of both States whether the provisions of the Constitutions of the Arab and Jewish States in Palestine dealing therewith and the religious rights appertaining thereto are being properly applied and respected.

(c) The Governor shall also be empowered to make decisions on the basis of existing rights in cases of disputes which may arise between the different religious communities or the rights of a religious community in respect of the Holy Places, religious buildings and sites in any part of Palestine.

In this task he may be assisted by a consultative council of representatives of different denominations acting in an advisory capacity.

D. *Duration of the Special Regime*

The Statute elaborated by the Trusteeship Council on the aforementioned principles shall come into force not later than 1 October 1948. It shall remain in force in the first instance for a period of ten years, unless the Trusteeship Council finds it necessary to undertake a re-examination of these provisions at an earlier date. After the expiration of this period the whole scheme shall be subject to re-examination by the Trusteeship Council in the light of the experience acquired with its functioning. The residents of the City shall be free to express by means of a referendum their wishes as to possible modifications of the regime of the City.

Part IV. Capitulations

States whose nationals have in the past enjoyed in Palestine the privileges and immunities of foreigners, including the benefits of consular jurisdiction and protection, as formerly enjoyed by capitulation or usage in the Ottoman Empire, are invited to renounce any right pertaining to them to the re-establishment of such privileges and immunities in the proposed Arab and Jewish States and the City of Jerusalem.

Appendix C: Resolution 242 (1967) of 22 November 1967

The Security Council,

Expressing its continuing concern with the grave situation in the Middle East,

Emphasizing the inadmissibility of the acquisition of territory by war and the need to work for a just and lasting peace in which every State in the area can live in security,

Emphasising further that all Member States in their acceptance of the Charter of the United Nations have undertaken a commitment to act in accordance with Article 2 of the Charter,

1. *Affirms* that the fulfilment of Charter principles requires the establishment of a just and lasting peace in the Middle East which should include the application of both the following principles:

(i) Withdrawal of Israel armed forces from territories occupied in the recent conflict;

(ii) Termination of all claims or states of belligerency and respect for and acknowledgement of the sovereignty, territorial integrity and political independence of every State in the area and their right to live in peace within secure and recognized boundaries free from threats or acts of force;

2. *Affirms further* the necessity

(a) For guaranteeing freedom of navigation through international waterways in the area;

(b) For achieving a just settlement of the refugee problem;

(c) For guaranteeing the territorial inviolability and political independence of every State in the area, through measures including the establishment of demilitarized zones;

3. *Requests* the Secretary-General to designate a Special Representative to proceed to the Middle East to establish and maintain contacts with the States concerned in order to promote agreement and assist efforts

to achieve a peaceful and accepted settlement in accordance with the provisions and principles in this resolution;

4. *Requests* the Secretary-General to report to the Security Council on the progress of the efforts of the Special Representative as soon as possible.

Adopted unanimously at the 1332nd meeting.

Appendix D: Resolution 338 (1973) of 22 October 1973

The Security Council

1. *Calls upon* all parties to the present fighting to cease all firing and terminate all military activity immediately, no later than 12 hours after the moment of the adoption of this decision, in the positions they now occupy;

2. *Calls upon* the parties concerned to start immediately after the cease-fire the implementation of Security Council resolution 242 (1967) in all of its parts;

3. *Decides* that, immediately and concurrently with the cease-fire, negotiations shall start between the parties concerned under appropriate auspices aimed at establishing a just and durable peace in the Middle East.

Adopted at the 1747th meeting by 14 votes to none

Appendix E: UN Resolution 49/88 (Middle East Peace Process: The Positive Resolution)

The General Assembly,

Recalling General Assembly resolution 48/58 of 14 December 1993 and Economic and Social Council resolution 1994/29 of 27 July 1994,

Stressing that the achievement of a comprehensive, just and lasting settlement of the Middle East conflict will constitute a significant contribution to strengthening international peace and security,

Recalling the convening of the Peace Conference on the Middle East at Madrid on 30 October 1991, on the basis of Security Council resolutions 242 (1967) of 22 November 1967 and 338 (1973) of 22 October 1973, and the subsequent bilateral negotiations, as well as the meetings of the multilateral working groups, and noting with satisfaction the broad international support for the peace process,

Noting the continuing positive participation of the United Nations as a full extraregional participant in the work of the multilateral working groups,

Bearing in mind the Declaration of Principles on Interim Self-Government Arrangements, signed by the Government of the State of Israel and the Palestine Liberation Organization in Washington, D.C., on 13 September 1993, and the subsequent Agreement on the Gaza Strip and the Jericho Area, signed by the Government of the State of Israel and the Palestine Liberation Organization, the representative of the Palestinian people, at Cairo on 4 May 1994, and their 29 August 1994 agreement on the preparatory transfer of powers and responsibilities,

Also bearing in mind the Agreement between Israel and Jordan on the Common Agenda, signed in Washington, D.C., on 14 September 1993, the Washington Declaration, signed by Jordan and Israel on 25 July 1994, and the Jordan-Israel Treaty of Peace of 26 October 1994,

Welcoming the declaration of the Middle East/North Africa Economic Summit, held at Casablanca from 30 October to 1 November 1994,

1. *Welcomes* the peace process started at Madrid and supports the subsequent bilateral negotiations;

2. *Stresses* the importance of, and need for, achieving a comprehensive, just and lasting peace in the Middle East;

3. *Expresses its full support* for the achievements of the peace process thus far, in particular the Declaration of Principles on Interim Self-Government Arrangements signed by the Government of the State of Israel and the Palestine Liberation Organization, the subsequent Agreement on the Gaza Strip and the Jericho Area, signed by the Government of the State of Israel and the Palestine Liberation Organization, the representative of the Palestinian people, their 29 August 1994 agreement on the preparatory transfer of powers and responsibilities, the agreement between Israel and Jordan on the Common Agenda, the Washington Declaration, signed by Jordan and Israel on 25 July 1994, and the Jordan-Israel Treaty of Peace of 26 October 1994, which constitute important steps in achieving a comprehensive, just and lasting peace in the Middle East, and urges all parties to implement the agreements reached;

4. *Stresses* the need for achieving rapid progress on the other tracks of the Arab-Israeli negotiations within the peace process;

5. *Welcomes* the results of the Conference to Support Middle East Peace, convened in Washington, D.C., on 1 October 1993, including the establishment of the Ad Hoc Liaison Committee, and the subsequent work of the World Bank Consultative Group, welcomes also the appointment by the Secretary-General of the "United Nations Special Coordinator in the occupied territories", and urges Member States to expedite economic, financial and technical assistance to the Palestinian people during the interim period;

6. *Calls upon* all Member States also to extend economic, financial and technical assistance to parties in the region, and to render support for the peace process;

7. *Considers* that an active United Nations role in the Middle East peace process and in assisting in the implementation of the Declaration of Principles can make a positive contribution;

8. *Encourages* regional development and cooperation in the areas where work has begun within the framework of the Madrid Conference.

Adopted by the United Nations General Assembly on 16 December 1994 by a vote of 149 to 4 with 2 abstentions.

Appendix F: Main Points: The Interim Agreement between Israel and the PLO (Regarding Transfer of Power in the West Bank) Washington D.C., September 28, 1995

Background

The Interim Agreement between Israel and the PLO constitutes a new and important stage in the transition from conflict to reconciliation between Israel and the Palestinian people—as well as between Israel and the Arab states. The agreement is part of the peace process which began at Camp David, in 1978, with the ultimate aim of achieving peace in the whole region, and was resumed in October 1991 in Madrid. A breakthrough in Israeli-Palestinian relations was marked by the Declaration of Principles on Interim Self-government Arrangements of September 13, 1993. This declaration set out the principles which are to govern Israel-Palestinian relations for an interim period of five years, until the implementation of a permanent status agreement.

To date, preliminary agreements implemented pursuant to the Declaration of Principles include the Gaza-Jericho Agreement of May 4, 1994 which provided for the withdrawal of Israeli forces from the Gaza Strip and the Jericho Area and the transfer of civil powers in these areas to a Palestinian Authority, and subsequent agreements giving the Palestinian Authority limited responsibilities for additional civil spheres throughout the West Bank. All these agreements are superseded by the provisions of the Interim Agreement.

The main object of the Interim Agreement is to broaden Palestinian self-government in the West Bank by means of an elected self-governing authority—the Palestinian Council. This will allow the Palestinians to conduct their own internal affairs, reduce points of friction between Israelis and Palestinians, and open a new era of cooperation and coexistence based on common interest, dignity and mutual respect. At the same time it protects Israel's vital interests, and in particular its security interests, both with regard to external security as well as the personal security of its citizens in the West Bank.

General

The Interim Agreement between Israel and the PLO, including its various annexes, comprises some 400 pages, setting forth the future relations between Israel and the Palestinians. To the main body of the agreement are appended seven annexes dealing with: security arrangements, elections, civil affairs (transfer of powers), legal matters, economic relations, Israeli-Palestinian cooperation, and the release of Palestinian prisoners.

The agreement states that a Palestinian Council will be elected for an interim period not to exceed five years from the signing of the Gaza-Jericho Agreement (i.e., no later than May 1999). The negotiations on the permanent status arrangements will begin no later than May 1996.

The permanent status negotiations will deal with the remaining issues, including Jerusalem, refugees, settlements, security arrangements, borders, relations, and cooperation with neighboring countries, etc.

Elections

The Council is an elected body and, accordingly, the agreement sets out arrangements for democratic elections to the Council by all Palestinians of the West Bank and the Gaza Strip age 18 or over, who are registered in the population register. The elections will take place 22 days after the conclusion of an IDF redeployment from populated areas in the West Bank.

The elections to the Council will be personal and by district. A separate election will be held simultaneously for the election of the Head of the Executive Authority of the Council.

The candidacy of an individual, a party, or a coalition of parties shall be rejected if the said candidate, party, or coalition professes racist views or acts in an illegal or undemocratic manner.

Palestinian residents of Jerusalem will be able to participate in the elections according to special arrangements in the agreement. The voting will take place in localities outside Jerusalem and by means of special envelopes which will be sent from post offices to the Central Elections Committee. A Palestinian with a Jerusalem address who wishes to stand for election to the Palestinian Council will be able to do so only if he or she has an additional valid address in the West Bank or the Gaza Strip.

All stages of the election process will be open to international observation, to ensure that they are free and fair. At the request of the parties, the European Union has agreed to coordinate the election observation. The observer delegation will be composed of representatives from the following states and international organizations: the EU, the UN, the USA, the Russian Federation, Canada, Egypt, Japan, Jordan, Norway, South Africa, the Non-Aligned Nations, the OAU, the Islamic Conference Organization.

The Palestinian Council

The Palestinian Countil to be established following the elections will assume various powers and responsibilities in security and civil spheres in the West Bank and Gaza, as detailed below. With the establishment of the Council, the Israeli military government will be withdrawn and the Civil Administration dissolved. The Council will assume responsibility for all rights, liabilities, and obligations in the spheres transferred to it. At the same time Israel will retain those powers and responsibilities not transferred to the Council.

The Council, which will have 82 members, will have legislative and executive powers. The agreement provides that the legislative powers will be exercised by the Council as a whole, while its executive powers will be exercised by a committee of the Council—the Executive Authority. This committee shall comprise Council members together with a small number of appointed officials.

The powers of the Council will extend to all matters within its jurisdiction. It should be noted that it will not have powers in the sphere of foreign relations. The agreement does, however, provide for a number of areas in which the PLO may, on behalf of the Council, conduct negotiations and sign agreements (economic, donor countries, regional development).

Security and Redeployment

The IDF will redeploy in the West Bank according to the timetable set out in the agreement. In the first stage, designed to facilitate the holding of elections, the IDF will withdraw from the populated areas of the West Bank: the six cities—Jenin, Nablus, Tulkarem, Kalkilya, Ramallah, and Bethlehem (in the city of Hebron special security arrangements will apply as provided in the agreement)—and 450 towns and villages. At the end of this redeployment, there will be almost no IDF presence in Palestinian population centers.

In general, throughout the West Bank and the Gaza Strip, Israel will have overall responsibility for external security and the security of Israelis and settlements.

With regard to internal security and public order, the agreement establishes different arrangements for three types of area:

—Area "A" comprises the six cities listed above. In these areas, the Palestinian Council will have full responsibility for internal security and public order, as well as full civil responsibilities.

—Area "B" comprises the Palestinian towns and villages of the West Bank. In these areas, which contain some 68 percent of the Palestinian population, the Council will be granted full civil authority, as in Area "A". The Council will be charged with maintaining public order, while Israel will have overall security authority to safeguard its citizens and to combat terrorism. This responsibility shall take precedence over the Palestinian responsibility for public order.

Palestinian police stations will be established in specified towns and villages to enable the Palestinian police to exercise its responsibility for public order. The agreement contains provisions requiring that the movement of Palestinian police be coordinated and confirmed with Israel.

—In Area "C", which comprises the unpopulated areas, areas of strategic importance to Israel and the Jewish settlements, Israel will retain full responsibility for security and public order. The Council will assume all those civil responsibilities not related to terrory, such as economics, health, education, etc.

Further Redeployments

In addition to the redeployment of Israeli military forces described above, the agreement provides that a series of further redeployments are to take place at six-month intervals following the inauguration of the Council. In the course of these redeployments, additional parts of Area C will be transferred to the territorial jurisdiction of the Council, so that by the completion of the redeployment phases, Palestinian territorial jurisdiction will cover West Bank territory except for the areas where jurisdiction is to be determined under the final status negotiations (settlements, military locations, etc.).

The Revocation of the PLO Convenant

The agreement contains an undertaking to revoke those articles of the Palestinian Covenant calling for the destruction of Israel, within two months of the inauguration of the Council.

Provided by the Ministry of Foreign Affairs of the State of Israel.

Appendix G: Israel's Diplomatic Relations

Countries That Have Recently Established Diplomatic Relations with Israel

Since October 1992

Nicaragua	October 1992
Eritrea	May 1993
Vietnam	July 1993
Mozambique	July 1993

Since September 1993 (Signing of the Declaration of Principles)

Gabon	September 1993
Mauritius	September 1993
Burkina Faso	October 1993
Cambodia	October 1993
Turkmenistan	October 1993
Sao Tome & Principe	November 1993
Zimbabwe	November 1993
Vanuatu	December 1993
Botswana	December 1993
Holy See (Vatican)	December 1993
Laos	December 1993
Madagascar	January 1994
Equatorial Guinea	January 1994
Namibia	February 1994
Guinea-Bissau	March 1994
Andorra	May 1994
Uganda	July 1994
Cape Verde	July 1994
Ghana	August 1994
Senegal	August 1994
Morocco (Liaison Offices)	September 1994
Tunisia (Liaison Officers)	October 1994
Jordan	October 1994
Rwanda	October 1994
Palau	October 1994

Comoros	November 1994
Nauru	December 1994
Tanzania	February 1995
Burundi	March 1995

Countries with Which Israel Has Diplomatic Relations 25 July 1995

1. Albania
2. Andorra[1]
3. Angola
4. Antigua and Barbuda
5. Argentina
6. Armenia
7. Australia
8. Austria
9. Azerbaijan
10. Bahamas
11. Barbados
12. Belarus
13. Belgium
14. Belize
15. Benin
16. Bolivia
17. Botswana[1]
18. Brazil
19. Bulgaria
20. Burkina Faso[1]
21. Burundi
22. Cambodia[1]
23. Cameroon
24. Canada
25. Cape Verde[1]
26. Central African Republic
27. Chile
28. China
29. Colombia
30. Comoros[1]
31. Congo
32. Costa Rica
33. Côte D'Ivoire
34. Cyprus
35. Czech Republic
36. Denmark
37. Dominica
38. Dominican Republic
39. Ecuador
40. Egypt
41. El Salvador
42. Equatorial Guinea[1]
43. Eritrea
44. Estonia
45. Ethiopia
46. Fiji
47. Finland
48. France
49. Gabon[1]
50. Gambia
51. Georgia
52. Germany
53. Ghana[1]
54. Greece
55. Grenada
56. Guatemala
57. Guinea-Bissau[1]
58. Guyana
59. Haiti
60. Honduras
61. Hungary
62. Iceland
63. India
64. Ireland
65. Italy
66. Jamaica
67. Japan
68. Jordan[1]
69. Kazakhstan
70. Kenya
71. Kiribati[2]
72. Kyrgyzstan

73. Laos[1]
74. Latvia
75. Lesotho
76. Liberia
77. Liechtenstein
78. Lithuania
79. Luxembourg
80. Madagascar[1]
81. Malawi
82. Malta
83. Marshall Islands
84. Mauritius[1]
85. Mexico
86. Micronesia
87. Moldova
88. Monaco
89. Mongolia
90. Morocco[1,3]
91. Mozambique
92. Myanmar
93. Namibia[1]
94. Nauru[1,2]
95. Nepal
96. Netherlands
97. New Zealand
98. Nicaragua
99. Nigeria
100. Norway
101. Palau[1,2]
102. Panama
103. Papua New Guinea
104. Paraguay
105. Peru
106. Philippines
107. Poland
108. Portugal
109. Romania
110. Russian Federation
111. Rwanda[1]
112. S. Korea
113. Saint Kitts & Nevis
114. Saint Lucia
115. Samoa
116. San Marino
117. São Tomé & Príncipe[1]
118. Senegal[1]
119. Seychelles
120. Sierra Leone
121. Singapore
122. Slovak Republic
123. Slovenia
124. Solomon Islands
125. South Africa
126. Spain
127. St. Vincent & The Grenadines
128. Suriname
129. Swaziland
130. Sweden
131. Switzerland[2] Observer
132. Tajikistan
133. Tanzania
134. Thailand
135. Togo
136. Tonga[2]
137. Trinidad and Tobago
138. Tunisia[1,3]
139. Turkey
140. Turkmenistan[1]
141. Tuvalu[2]
142. Uganda[1]
143. Ukraine
144. United Kingdom
145. United States
146. Uruguay
147. Uzbekistan
148. Vanuatu[1]
149. Vatican[1,2] Observer
150. Venezuela
151. Vietnam
152. Yugoslavia
153. Zaire
154. Zambia
155. Zimbabwe[1]

Countries with Which Israel Does Not Have Diplomatic Relations 25 July 1995

1. Afghanistan
2. Algeria
3. Bahrain
4. Bangladesh
5. Bhutan
6. Bosnia and Herzegovina
7. Brunei Darussalam
8. Chad
9. Croatia
10. Cuba
11. Djibouti
12. Guinea
13. Indonesia
14. Iran
15. Iraq
16. Kuwait
17. Lebanon
18. Libya
19. Macedonia (F.Y.R.M.)
20. Malaysia
21. Maldives
22. Mali
23. Mauritania
24. Niger
25. North Korea (D.P.R.K.)
26. Oman
27. Pakistan
28. Qatar
29. Saudi Arabia
30. Somalia
31. Sri Lanka
32. Sudan
33. Syria
34. United Arab Emirates
35. Yemen

[1]Established relations after the signing of the Declaration of Principles (13 September 1993).

[2]Not a United Nations Member State.

[3]Partial diplomatic relations established.